Twayne's English Authors Series

EDITOR OF THIS VOLUME

Bertram H. Davis

Florida State University

Sir Samuel Garth

TEAS 276

Painting by Godfrey Kneller
Courtesy of National Portrait Gallery, London

Sir Samuel Garth

SIR SAMUEL GARTH

By RICHARD I. COOK

Kent State University

TWAYNE PUBLISHERS
A DIVISION OF G.K. HALL & CO., BOSTON

Copyright © 1980 by G. K. Hall & Co.

Published in 1980 by Twayne Publishers,
A Division of G. K. Hall & Co.
All Rights Reserved

Printed on permanent/durable acid-free paper and bound
in the United States of America

First Printing

Library of Congress Cataloging in Publication Data

Cook, Richard I
Sir Samuel Garth.

(Twayne's English authors series ; TEAS 276)
Bibliography: p. 162-65
Includes index.
1. Garth, Samuel, Sir, 1661-1719—
Criticism and interpretation.
PR3471.G3C6   821'.5   79-13360
ISBN 0-8057-6775-4

Contents

    About the Author
    Preface
    Chronology
1. Life of Garth   11
2. *The Dispensary:* The Historical and Literary Background   46
3. *The Dispensary* as a Poem   75
4. The Other Works   99
5. Garth's Influence and Reputation   125
    Notes and References   137
    Selected Bibliography   162
    Index   166

About the Author

Richard I. Cook is currently Professor of English at Kent State University in Ohio, where his field of specialization is eighteenth century English literature. He received his B. A. and M. A. degrees from Washington University (St. Louis) and his Ph.D. degree from the University of California at Berkeley. Prior to his present position at Kent State, he has taught at Rutgers University and at the University of Washington.

Professor Cook's major scholarly concern has been with the English writers—particularly the satirists—of the earlier portion of the eighteenth century, and he has published numerous articles on Swift, Pope, Defoe, Mandeville, and others in professional journals. He is the author of *Jonathan Swift as a Tory Pamphleteer* (University of Washington Press, 1967), a detailed study of Swift's work as a polemicist for the Harley-St. John ministry of 1710-1714. In 1973 he edited Bernard Mandeville's *A Modest Defence of Publick Stews* (1724) for the Augustan Reprint Society of the William Andrews Clark Memorial Library of the University of California at Los Angeles (Publication Number 162). And in 1974 he published his full-length study *Bernard Mandeville*, Twayne English Authors Series Number 170.

Preface

Authors of books about once famous but currently obscure poets share an understandable tendency to justify their labors by magnifying the importance of their subjects and bemoaning the "undeserved neglect" into which they have fallen. Doubtless I have sinned in this direction, for which I have all the less excuse, since Garth himself is on record as saying:

> I am not of an opinion . . . to think that one is under an obligation to extol every thing he finds in the author he undertakes: I am sure one is no more obliged to do so, than a painter is to make every face, that sits to him, handsome. It is enough if he sets the best features he finds in their full and most advantageous light. But if the poet has private deformities, though good-breeding will not allow to expose him naked, yet surely there can be no reason to recommend him, as the most finished model of harmony and proportion. (Preface to Ovid's *Metamorphoses*).

It is the burden of this study that Sir Samuel Garth, though not the "finished model of harmony and proportion" so many of his contemporaries thought him, is nonetheless a much better poet than his latter-day eclipse would suggest. As an author who helped to formulate and establish one of the dominant poetic forms of his century, as a physician who played a central role in a pioneering effort to provide medical services to the London poor, and as a man whose wit and benevolence made him the personal friend (and sometimes the mentor) of many of the most famous writers of his day, Garth may fairly claim the attention of readers interested in the social and literary history of eighteenth-century England. It is in the hope of acquainting more such readers with Garth the man and the artist that the present volume is offered.

RICHARD I. COOK

Kent State University

Chronology

1661	Samuel Garth, son of William Garth of Bolam, Durham, is born.
1676	May 27, Garth is admitted to Peterhouse, Cambridge, as pensioner.
1679	Receives B.A. from Cambridge.
1684	Receives M.A. from Cambridge.
1687	Studies medicine at University of Leyden.
1688–1689	Travels on Continent.
1691	July 7, receives M.D. from Cambridge. Sometime in early 1690s marries Martha, daughter of Sir Henry Beaufoy.
1692	June 25, admitted as candidate to Royal College of Physicians.
1693	June 26, elected fellow of the College of Physicians.
1694	Delivers Gulstonian Lecture "De Respiratione" before College of Physicians.
1697	September 17, delivers Harveian Oration before College of Physicians; published soon after.
1699	May, publishes *The Dispensary*; second and third editions in the same year.
1700	May 13, delivers eulogy at Dryden's funeral; publishes translation of Plutarch's "Life of Otho"; fourth edition of *The Dispensary*.
1702	Publishes translation of Demosthenes's "First Philippick"; elected censor of the College of Physicians.
1703	About this time, joins the Kit-Cat Club; fifth edition of *The Dispensary*.
1706	Elected fellow of Royal Society; sixth edition of *The Dispensary*.
1710	Publishes "To the Earl of Godolphin"; daughter, Martha, elopes with Colonel William Boyle.
1711	Publishes *Epitaphium Lucretii Editionis*; visits Marlborough on Continent.

1713 Writes epilogue to Addison's *Cato*.
1714 October 11, Garth is knighted; seventh edition of *The Dispensary*.
1715 May 2, publishes *Claremont;* appointed physician-in-ordinary to King George I; appointed physician-general to the army.
1715 Leaves for Italy in mid-1715; on return, in fall of 1716, stops in Paris to see Bolingbroke.
1717 Publishes edition of Ovid's *Metamorphoses;* wife, Martha, dies.
1718 Visits Paris; eighth edition of *The Dispensary*.
1719 January 18, dies in London; buried at St. Mary's Church, Harrow-on-the-Hill.

CHAPTER 1

Life of Garth

VERY nearly all the information that has come down to us concerning the birth and early years of Sir Samuel Garth is contained in the brief notation made in the Peterhouse register at Cambridge when Garth was admitted as a pensioner. From that entry of May 27, 1676, we learn that Samuel Garth was the eldest son of William Garth of Bolam, Durham, that he attended school at Ingleton, and that at the time of admittance he was sixteen years old. In 1938 William Cornog examined the parish records for the district within which Bolam lies, but could find no specific mention of Samuel Garth, though he did discover an entry for the baptism (on September 29, 1664) of Samuel's brother, Thomas.[1] A clearer picture of Garth's family emerges from his father's will, where Samuel is identified as the eldest of three sons—the youngest being the aforementioned Thomas, and the middle son his father's namesake, William. It was to the latter, rather than to his firstborn, that the senior Garth left the bulk of his estate, giving as his reason that he had already ".been at great charges in the education of his eldest son, Samuel Garth, at the University of Cambridge, and in his taking his degree there as Doctor of Physick."[2]

The "great charges" incurred by Garth's education must have derived, at least in part, from its unusually long duration; for he did not complete work on his M.D. from Cambridge until some fifteen years after his entry. Garth received his B.A. degree in 1679 and his M.A. in 1684. but between that year and 1691, when he was awarded his doctorate of medicine, Garth spent two separate periods in travel on the Continent. During the first of these, according to William Munk, Garth enrolled as a medical student at the University of Leyden in 1687.[3] That Garth spent at least some of his time abroad pursuing his studies is confirmed by two references of 1692. In the first of these, when Garth was examined in pathology (on March 18) as part of his application for admission to the Royal College of Physicians, he was described in the college *Annals* as "haveing spent some years in forreign campaignes & Hospitalls."[4] And later that year when Garth was recommended by the college for special duty at Portsmouth, his experience "in foreign hospitals" was cited as a particular qualification.[5] The earlier reference to "forreign campaignes" suggests military service, but if such was the case, no corroborating evidence has survived.

Soon after this educational excursion to the Continent, Garth undertook a second trip, the purpose of which is much more mysterious. In the *State Papers* for January 24, 1698, there is included a "Warrant for a license to SAMUEL GARTH, doctor of physick, who went into the French King's dominions, since 11th December 1688, without license, . . . to stay in England or other [of] the King's dominions."[6] That he should have left England—evidently in some haste, since he did not obtain a license—at almost the precise time that the Catholic James II was forced to flee to France, implies that Garth may have been among the exiled king's supporters. This implication approaches open assertion in the records of the House of Lords for February 9, 1703, where we find Garth's name at the head of a list of "persons who had licenses in the reign of William III to return into England . . . to prevent correspondence with the late King James. . . ."[7]

If, as the uncertain evidence indicates, Garth was indeed a youthful adherent of the Pretender's cause, that allegiance clearly could not have gone very deep; nor did it last for very long. That Garth embraced Roman Catholicism just before his death, we have the unconfirmed report of Alexander Pope (discussed below), though even Pope does not deny the prior religious skepticism which earned Garth a widespread reputation for atheism. Still more than his religious sentiments, Garth's subsequent politics are strongly at odds with any early advocacy of the Jacobite cause; for throughout his public career he was to remain a conspicuously dedicated Whig and outspoken Hanoverian whose greatest heroes were William III and the duke of Marlborough. Given the suggestive, but inconclusive evidence, we cannot be sure whether Garth did, in fact, briefly support James II; but at least one thing is clear: if he did, he kept the secret from his contemporaries remarkably well, since in all the bitter personal attacks that his medical, political, and literary enemies directed against him, there is no whisper of so potentially embarrassing an accusation.

Whatever the reasons for Garth's 1688 trip to the Continent, by 1691 he was back in Cambridge, where on July 7 he received his M.D. We may assume that soon thereafter he went to London to establish a practice, since we find that on June 25, 1692, he became a candidate for the Royal College of Physicians, and almost exactly one year later, on June 26, 1693, he was formally admitted as a fellow. Garth seems to have impressed his professional colleagues from the very first. As noted earlier, in December 1692, while he was still only a candidate for membership, the fellows of the College recommended him to the Lords of the Admiralty for special service at Portsmouth. A further indication of esteem came in March of 1694, when Garth served as Gulstonian lecturer before the College. The title of his lectures was "De Respiratione," and so well were they received that on March 8 the "President and Censors desired Dr. Garth to print his lectures, which he promised to do in Latin."[8] Unfortunately, Garth did not keep that promise, and the text of this, his only medical work, has not survived.

A more significant honor came to Garth in 1697, when he was selected to deliver the annual Harveian Oration before the College of Physicians. In 1656, William Harvey, famous for his discovery of the circulation of the blood, had bequeathed his estate to the college with the stipulation that part of the income be used in support of an annual Latin oration before the assembled members. That Garth should receive so prestigious an assignment indicates how high a reputation he had earned in his little more than four years as a member of the college. On September 17, 1697, *"to the great satisfaction of the* audience, *and his own* reputation,"[9] Garth delivered his *Oratio Laudatoria in Aedibus Collegii Regalis Med. Lond.*, and shortly thereafter the work—Garth's first known publication[10]—was printed.

Perhaps the most noteworthy feature of Garth's Harveian Oration is the lavishness of the "beautiful Elogium introduc'd into it of King William."[11] In his bequest, Harvey had suggested that a portion of each address be devoted to commemoration of the college benefactors. This injunction Garth liberally follows, most particularly with regard to the king, whose praises occupy more than half of the entire text. Garth hails William as "not only the Guardian of This Colledge, but the deliverer of the Christian world and the Restorer of publick Peace."[12] Only nine years after his putative flight into exile with the Pretender, Garth leaves no room for doubt as to his unequivocally Protestant sentiments concerning the Glorious Revolution. Apostrophizing William directly, Garth describes the expulsion of James II as an occasion when "England[,] languishing and haveing her publick safety shaken[,] courted you a fresh to be her Saviour, and into your bossom fled for shelter; It was not your Ambition but our necessitie that made you King here: by your bare presence you restored great Brittain. . . ."[13]

In the final paragraphs of his Harveian Oration Garth touches briefly upon a subject which had already divided the College of Physicians for over two decades—namely, the advisability of establishing a charity clinic to treat indigent patients. In this, his initial public pronouncement on the subject, Garth firmly endorses the proposed "Repositorie well furnished with Druggs for the help of the Poor," and he goes on to characterize those opposed to the plan as avaricious persons "unto whom all is fish that comes to their Net; who haveing neither Learning nor good Manners . . . attempt to Subvert this Fabrick. . . ."[14] It was to be less than two years after these remarks that Garth would address himself to the subject more definitively in *The Dispensary*, a work which at the time of the Harveian Oration may well have been in progress.

I *"The Men of Sense" Against "The Men of Wit"*

The dispute over establishment of a charity clinic for the London poor was merely one aspect of a larger and long-standing animosity between the Society of Apothecaries (which held legal authority for the preparation and sale of drugs in London) and the Royal College of Physicians (which by charter enjoyed a monopoly in the practice of medicine). Practically speaking, however, the physicians' monopoly could not be effectively enforced, and by the time of the Restoration, many apothecaries had begun openly to practice medicine, particularly among the poor. The professional acrimony thus created was heightened by the social antagonism with which the two groups faced each other. To many physicians, the apothecaries seemed little more than ill-educated tradesmen, scarcely distinguishable from the

Grocers Company with which prior to 1617 they had been formally incorporated. Conversely, the apothecaries naturally resented what they saw as the arrogance and self-importance by which physicians rejected all claimants to competence outside their own ranks. By the latter part of the seventeenth century the issue of a proposed charity clinic for the London poor (see chapter 2) had emerged as the symbolic focal point of each group's hostility toward the other.

As of 1699, Garth—though increasingly prominent in his profession—was a figure scarcely known outside medical circles. However, with the appearance in that year of *The Dispensary: A Poem*, Garth was elevated almost overnight to a position of eminence among the wits of the literary world. Garth's abrupt emergence as a poet seems all the more remarkable in that there is nothing in the known facts of his earlier career to suggest that he had either the ambition or the ability to win a reputation as an author. In the preface he added to the second edition, Garth speaks of poetry as "an amusement I have very little practised hitherto, nor perhaps ever shall again."[15] Given the technical skill and complexity of *The Dispensary*, Garth may well be exaggerating his inexperience, though no ascribable trace of his apprentice work, if any, has survived.

To its fledgling author, the immediate popularity of *The Dispensary* must have been gratifying. The first edition was advertised in the London *Post Boy* (May 6-8, 1699), and within little more than a month two further editions were required. Nor did the poem's popularity end with the timeliness of its subject matter. In the remaining twenty years of its author's lifetime, *The Dispensary* (with periodic additions and emendations) was to achieve eight legal and two pirated editions, and the poem continued to be regularly reissued, both individually and in collections, throughout the eighteenth century. Moreover, the critical response was overwhelmingly favorable.

As a partisan document on a controversial topic, however, the poem was not without disparagers, one of the most vociferous of whom proved to be Sir Richard Blackmore. Blackmore, like Garth, was both a poet and physician. In the first capacity, he had published two enormous epics, *Prince Arthur* (1695) and *King Arthur* (1697); while, as a doctor, he had allied himself with the antidispensarian faction in the College of Physicians. Garth, who respected neither Blackmore's verse nor his medical politics, satirized both in canto 4 of *The Dispensary*, where Blackmore figures as the "Bard." Blackmore quickly responded with *A Satyr Against Wit*, in which Garth and all "the little loitt'ring Fry/ That follow *Garth*"[16] are ridiculed. Blackmore's complaints, however, were not limited to the dispensary issue: in a larger sense, Garth and his poem are treated as mere symptoms of a widespread cultural malaise ascribable to John Dryden, whose debased pursuit of "Wit," in Blackmore's view, had taught a whole generation of poets to mock both religion and virtue.

Blackmore's attack, naturally, did not go long unanswered: in March, 1700, there appeared a collection of mock panegyrics entitled *Commendatory Verses on the Author of the Two Arthurs and the Satyr Against Wit*. Dryden was then not far from death, and he does not seem to have participated directly in the *Commendatory Verses*, though it is likely he was kept informed of the work's progress. Among the better known of the poets who took part in this venture were Sir Charles Sedley, Henry Blount, Sir Richard Steele, and William Walsh. Of the forty-one poems comprising this collection, Garth himself contributed "To the Merry Poetaster at Sadlers-Hall, in Cheapside." Inevitably, Blackmore and his allies mounted a counterattack, which took the form of a collection of *Discommendatory Verses, on Those Which are Truly Commendatory, on the Author of the Two Arthurs and the Satyr against Wit*. In the course of this pamphlet war between the "Men of Wit" and the "Men of Sense" Garth's name became firmly linked with Dryden's; and so it is perhaps only fitting that when Dryden died—some three weeks after the publication of the *Discommendatory Verses*—Garth assumed the role of major eulogist at the funeral.

II *Dryden's Funeral*

Exactly how well Dryden and Garth may have known each other personally is not certain, though Malone names Garth as one of the group of young admirers who spent many hours in the elder poet's company.[17] A relationship of a possibly closer sort is implied by Charles Boyle (earl of Orrery) in "To Dr. Garth, Upon the Dispensary," one of the prefatory verses added to the second edition. In this poem Boyle finds his own "poor feeble Muse" unqualified to praise Garth's work adequately, since "Artists alone should venture to commend / What Dennis can't condemn, nor Dryden mend."[18] The reference suggests, albeit ambiguously, that Dryden (like John Dennis) may have been one of those to whom *The Dispensary* was submitted before publication. Whether or not Dryden saw the work in manuscript, he did read it, and in one of the last poems he wrote, "To My Honour'd Kinsman, John Driden" (1699), he recorded his esteem for *"Garth,* gen'rous as his Muse"[19] and for the dispensarian cause.

Conversely, Garth's admiration and respect for Dryden—to whose translation of Vergil (1697) he was a subscriber—is apparent in the flattering references found in *The Dispensary* and elsewhere in his work, most particularly in his preface to Ovid's *Metamorphoses* (1717):

I cannot pass by that admirable English poet, without endeavouring to make his country sensible of the obligations they have to his Muse. Whether they consider the flowing grace of his versification; the vigorous sallies of his fancy; or the peculiar delicacy of his periods; they will discover excellencies never to be enough admired. If they trace him from the first productions of his youth to the last performances of his age, they will find, that as the tyranny of rhyme never imposed on the perspicuity of the sense; so a languid sense never wanted to be set off by the harmony of rhyme.[20]

On May 1, 1700, when Dryden died, his impoverished family arranged a simple burial in St. Anne's, Soho. However, a subscription was soon raised for a more imposing public ceremony and interment in Westminster Abbey. Toward this end the body was embalmed and taken on May 6 to the hall of the College of Physicians in Warwick Lane, where it lay in state for a week. Tradition has it that it was Garth who originally proposed the funeral subscription and then arranged for the lying in state;[21] the college *Annals,* however, mention only "several persons of quality" as involved.[22] Whatever his role in the arrangements, Garth's prominence in the ceremony itself is clear: for as the *Post Boy* reported in its May 9 announcement of the plans, the Latin eulogy was assigned to "that learned Physician and famous Orator," Dr. Samuel Garth.

In light of the conflicting testimony concerning its character, it is unfortunate that no copy of Garth's eulogy has survived. Dryden's burial and attendant obsequies took place on May 13, and in its account of the events the *Post Boy* of May 14 commends

Garth for his "eloquent oration in Latin in praise of the Deceased." Ned Ward offers a fuller account of the occasion, describing how ". . . the Famous Doctor G*[ar]th* ascended the Pulpit, where the Physicians make their Lectures, and deliver'd, according to the *Roman* Custom a Funeral Oration in *Latin* on his Deceased Friend; which he perform'd with great Approbation and Applause of all such Gentlemen that heard him, and were true Judges of the matter; Most Rhetorically setting forth those Elogies and Encomiums which no Poet hitherto, but the Great *Dryden,* could ever truly deserve."[23]

Also present at the ceremony was the playwright, George Farquhar, who, though he thought the music unseemly and the funeral procession chaotic, nevertheless had high praise for Garth's performance. In a letter to "Penelope," Farquhar says:

I come now from Mr. *Dryden's* Funeral, where we had an Ode in *Horace* Sung, instead of *David's* Psalms; whence you may find, that we don't think a Poet worth Christian Burial; the Pomp of the Ceremony was a kind of Rhapsody, and fitter, I think, for *Hudibras* than him; because the Cavalcade was mostly Burlesque; but he was an extraordinary Man, and bury'd after an extraordinary Fashion; for I do believe there was never such another Burial seen; the Oration indeed was great and ingenious, worthy the Subject, and like the Author, whose Prescriptions can restore the Living, and his Pen embalm the Dead.[24]

Other spectators, however, were less impressed by Garth. Edward Hinton, writing to a friend on May 14, says: "Dr. Garth made a Latin speech, and threw away some words and a great deal of false Latin in praise of the poet."[25] And a quarter of a century later in 1726, Thomas Hearne recalled the event as follows:

Mr. John Dryden . . . was buried in Westminster Abbey . . . in May, 1700, being carried from the College of Physicians, where an Oration was pronounced by the famous Dr. Garth, in which he did not mention one Word of Jesus Xt, but made an Oration as an Apostrophe to the Great God Apollo, to influence the Minds of the Auditors with a wise, but without doubt, Poetical Understanding, and, as a Conclusion, instead of a Psalm of David, repeated the 30th Ode of the 3rd Book of Horace's Odes, beginning, *Exegi Monumentum,* &c. He made a great many Blunders in the Pronunciation.[26]

Life of Garth

Both Garth and Dryden were well supplied with enemies only too happy to exaggerate the alleged improprieties of the funeral and to ridicule Garth's role in it. Thus, Tom Brown published in 1700 a "Description of Mr. Dryden's Funeral," in which he writes of Garth's oration:

> But stay my muse, the learned Garth appears,
> He sighing comes, and is half drowned in tears;
> The famous Garth whom learned poets call
> Knight of the order of the urinal.
> He of Apollo learnt his wondrous skill,
> He taught him how to sing and how to kill;
> For all he sends unto the darksome grave
> He honours also with an epitaph. . . .[27]

Similarly, in an anonymous poem of 1710 Satan is pictured as delivering greetings sent by his subjects in hell to their living friends. Among other messages, we learn that *"John Dryden, with his Bretheren of the Bays, / His love to Garth, Blaspheming Garth conveys, / And thanks him for his Pagan Funeral Praise."*[28]

These and other scurrilous versions of Dryden's funeral gave rise to a tradition that in one form or another persisted throughout the eighteenth century—namely, that Dryden's last rites had turned into a drunken, irreligious revel and that Garth (who in one variation delivers his oration from atop a beer barrel) was one of the worst offenders. Despite their absurdity, such stories did not fully disappear from Dryden's biographies until 1800, when Malone conclusively demonstrated their falsity.[29]

Whatever the cavils and inventions of his enemies, Garth's role in Dryden's funeral only emphasized a kinship which had already made him seem to many the logical heir apparent to the poetical throne left vacant by the elder poet's death. In the concluding poem of *Luctus Britannici: or the Tears of the British Muses: for the Death of John Dryden, Esq.* (1700), the editors—Henry Playford and Abel Roper—address Garth as Dryden's artistic legatee:

> Permit us then, our Dutious Zeal to prove,
> And make a Tender of our Tears and Love,
> As we with Sighs unfeign'd the Task pursue,
> And Weep him *Dead*, who still must Live in You.[30]

A generation later, Walter Harte in *An Essay on Satire* (1730), expresses the same idea when, after lamenting Dryden's death, he remarks: "His Spirit ceas'd not (in strict truth) to be; / For dying *Dryden* breath'd, O *Garth!* on thee."[31] So clear did the line of succession seem, that even the anonymous author of the *Epistle to Sr. Richard Blackmore* (1700)—who approved of neither Garth nor Dryden—was willing to concede the pedigree:

> Tho *Con[greve]* may in time, when he has merit,
> The Prophet's [i.e., Dryden's] Throne in peaceful sway inherit,
> The Poets all with one consent agree
> His mantle falls to *G[arth]* by Destiny,
> Who did whilst living wear his Livery.[32]

III *The Kit-Cat Club and Important Friends*

Nothing in Garth's subsequent behavior suggests that he ever took such inflated assessments of his poetic importance seriously, though he found obvious pleasure in the literary reputation *The Dispensary* won for him. In the opening years of the eighteenth century he enhanced that reputation with further publications. In 1700 the fourth edition of *The Dispensary* appeared, and in the same year Garth contributed the "Life of Otho" to a new translation of Plutarch's *Lives of the Noble Grecians and Romans.* He likewise played an unspecified role in the translation of Cervantes's *Don Quixote* published in four volumes between 1700 and 1704 by Pierre Motteux: in his preface to volume 1 Motteaux cites his debt to *"some other Gentlemen, who are not only Masters of the Spanish, but of the Delicacies of our Tongue. I have also Acknowledgements to pay to Mr.* Wycherly, *Mr.* Congreve, *Dr.* Garth. . . ."[33] In addition to these works, in 1702 Garth translated the "first Philippick" in *Several Orations of Demosthenes,* as well as contributing a brief "Anacreontic to Mr. Gay" to Charles Gildon's *Examen Miscellaneum.*

The translations of Plutarch and Demosthenes were both published by Jacob Tonson, who was thereafter to be Garth's lifelong publisher and personal friend. Just how early Garth and Tonson came to know each other is impossible to say. The fact that *The Dispensary* was first issued by John Nutt—who continued as publisher until his death in 1710, when Tonson took over—indicates that Tonson and Garth did not become well-acquainted until after 1699. Whatever the date of its inception, the new friendship was an important one for Garth. For Tonson was more than just a prominent publisher: he was also one of the founders and leading members of the famous Kit-Cat Club, into whose ranks he soon brought Garth. The Kit-Cat Club, which had been founded some time before the turn of the century, probably took its curious name from Christopher Catling, the pastry cook in whose shop the first meetings were held.[34] With a membership limited to thirty-nine, it became the most exclusive and best known of the political-literary societies of the day. From the beginning, the Kit-Cat Club had a heavily Whiggish and distinctly aristocratic cast, numbering among its early members such important figures as the Lords Dorset, Essex, Somerset, Sunderland, Somers, Marlborough, and Newcastle. Equally impressive to someone of Garth's tastes were the distinguished literary members, among them Joseph Addison, Richard Steele, William Congreve, John Vanbrugh, and (until he turned Tory in 1707) Matthew Prior. Into this imposing company, Garth—perhaps as early as 1700, but certainly no later than 1703—was introduced by Tonson.

Of all the friendships Garth acquired through the Kit-Cat Club, there was perhaps none he valued more than that of John and Sarah, duke and duchess of Marlborough. The duke's brilliant military victories on the Continent had made him a national hero; while his wife's equally brilliant espousal of the Whig cause at Queen Anne's court had turned her into a major political figure. Garth admired both lavishly, and there soon developed between them a relationship which—in light of the social distance involved—was remarkably close. Initially, the connection may have been primarily professional, for Garth was Marlborough's physician; before long, however, there existed a warm, personal friendship, which (at least on Garth's side) never seemed to slacken.

The degree of trust between the Marlboroughs and Garth is shown by the role he played in a highly sensitive family matter involving Charles Churchill, the duke's younger brother. Contemporary legal records and Marlborough family documents are mysteriously (or perhaps merely discreetly) silent on the subject, but two surviving letters by Garth to Sir Hans Sloane give us at least the outline of the incident. Neither letter is dated, but presumably both were written before Charles Churchill's retirement from London in 1708.

D^r D^r[:] I must beg of you to doe a good naturd thing in behalf of Cll Churchill. a Coachman that carry'd him, and was very rude[,] provokd him to give him 3 or 4 blows with a small stick. ye Man is since dead of a Plursisy and 4 Surgeons that open'd him have given their opinion that ye distemper and nothing else was ye occasion of his death. you were his Physician, and I would beg you acquaint ye Coroner's Jury with yor thoughts, which I dare say will be to acquitt Cll Churchill. in this you'll very much oblige Yo^r obedient serv^t[,] S. Garth.[35]

Garth's second letter on the subject indicates that the case, despite his efforts, was sent to trial by the Coroner's Jury. "Dr Doct^r[:] Let me beg you'll order yor affairs so as to bee at ye old Bayly to morrow at eight. I am sure all Cl Churchill's family will thank you for it. Hee is much esteemd by them all, and I am confident you think him innocent of what He is accus'd. I shall allways think my self oblig'd to you for doing him this peice of service, who am Yo^r obedient Servt S. Garth."[36] In the absence of further documentation or any record of legal disposition, it seems probable that the trial was either called off or resulted in dismissal of the charges.

Garth's admiration for the Marlboroughs is evident not only in his personal services to them, but in the praise of the duke he added to later editions of *The Dispensary*. In private conversation, he was no less outspokenly enthusiastic over the duchess, if we can believe one unflattering contemporary account. As the duchess's biographer puts it:

[Garth], who seems from the first to have been dumbfounded by Sarah's beauty, was happy to remain so for the rest of his life. His championship was unquestioning if not glorious. Not very articulate, he is chanced on at a patient's dinner-table where, "like one who is forst from the power of truth & the aboundance of his hart, & after he had been silant for a good while, lay down his knife & with a solom aserveration sayd the Duchess of Marlborough was the best woman in the world, the most generous & compassionate & ready to do good when any cause was rightly represented to her, & he pondered how one of so much merit ever came to be a favorit. . . ."[37]

Considering Garth's steadfast devotion, it is not surprising that during the Tory ascendancy, when the Marlboroughs moved abroad in 1712, the duchess showed a special affection for Garth in her distribution of farewell gifts. "The Duchess of Marlborough," reports Lord Berkeley, "hath given great presents at her taking leave of her friends, severall fine diamond rings & other jewells of great value, to Dr. Garth for one."[38] Writing on the same occasion to Viscount Fermanagh, Ralph Palmer describes the duchess' gift to Garth as "a diamond ring of [£]200 value."[39]

In the early years of the century Garth also developed numerous literary friendships, the most significant of which was with the young Alexander Pope. While still an adolescent, Pope met "Well-natur'd *Garth,*" for whose "early praise"[40] the precocious younger poet was grateful. Pope responded with a respect and friendship that found repeated expression over the years. Thus Garth was one of those to whom Pope submitted the manuscript of his *Pastorals,*[41] and, when the work was published in 1709, he dedicated "Summer" to Garth:

> Accept, O *Garth,* the Muse's early Lays,
> That adds this Wreath of Ivy to thy Bays;
> Hear what from Love unpractis'd Hearts endure,
> From Love, the sole Disease thou canst not cure![42]

To these lines, Pope later added the note: "Dr. *Samuel Garth,* Author of the *Dispensary,* was one of the first friends of the author, whose acquaintance with him began at fourteen or fifteen. Their friendship continu'd from the year 1703, to . . . his death."[43]

Particularly endearing to Pope was Garth's early enthusiasm for *The Rape of the Lock.* After the poem's first appearance in 1712, when Pope (against the advice of Addison and others) was considering an enlarged version, it was Garth who most strongly encouraged him to recast the poem into a fuller mock-epic form. Recalling the occasion in later years, Pope said: "The machinery [of *The Rape of the Lock*] was added afterwards to make it look a little more considerable; and the scheme of adding it was much liked and approved of by several of my friends, and particularly by Dr. Garth, who, as he was one of the best-natured men in the world, was very fond of it."[44]

Like his other writings, Pope's correspondence reflects his obvious affection for Garth. Ten years after Garth's death, for example, Pope, in a letter to Swift (November 28, 1729) writes: ". . . so I live; so shall I die; and hope one day to meet you, Bishop [Francis] Atterbury, poor [James] Craggs, Dr. Garth, Dean [George] Berkeley, and Mr. [Francis] Hutchenson, in that place, To which God of his infinite mercy brings us, and every body!"[45] Likewise, on June 7, 1732, he expresses his pleasure to Tonson for his gift of a portrait "of my old friend, Dr. Garth."[46] All in all, the frequency and warmth of such references— coupled with Garth's measurable influence on Pope's verse (see chapter 5)—unmistakably reflect the younger poet's genuinely high regard for the elder.

IV Poetical and Professional Career to 1710

The opening years of the eighteenth century were for Garth not only a time of social and literary success, but also a period of professional advancement. In 1700 Garth was one of the candidates considered for the prestigious post of "regius professor of physick" at his old university, Cambridge.[47] He did not receive the appointment, but in 1702 his colleagues in the College of Physicians elected him one of their four censors, whose job was "to survey, correct, and govern all physicians, or others that shall practise within their jurisdiction, and to fine and imprison for causes as they shall see cause."[48] In 1706 Garth was elected a fellow of the Royal Society, with whose secretary and later president, Sir Hans Sloane, he was personally and professionally close.[49] In the Sloane manuscripts in the British Library there are twelve undated letters by Garth to Sloane. These letters (excepting the two cited earlier) are mostly concerned with such matters as medical referrals, the arrangement of appointments, and requests for medical books.

As his professional reputation grew, Garth's practice flourished. The documentary record and the testimony of his contemporaries make it clear that Garth devoted a generous proportion of his time to serving the poor whose cause he had urged in *The Dispensary*. But at least as notable as his charity was the large number of eminent personages who employed his medical services. A list of Garth's famous patients would be very nearly as long as the list of his famous literary and political friends. Indeed, it would be much the same list, including such figures as Steele, Addison, the duke of Marlborough, the earl of

Wharton, Lady Mary Wortley Montagu, and Lord Grantham. After 1714 Garth's most illustrious patient was King George I, but prior to that Garth had already attended royalty. In the fall of 1708, when Queen Anne's consort, Prince George of Denmark fell ill (he was to die on October 28), one of his four physicians was Garth, who received £100 for his services.[50]

It is interesting to find that in treating Prince George, one of Garth's fellow doctors was his old poetical adversary, Sir Richard Blackmore. In their literary exchange nine years earlier, each man had denigrated the other's medical as well as poetical skills. However, such opinions, once the situation provoking them had passed, do not seem to have interfered with a cordial professional cooperation between the two men. On at least two subsequent occasions we find Garth and Blackmore in mutual attendance on a patient—though unfortunately both cases, like that of Prince George, proved terminal. In 1712 the two doctors collaborated in treating the final illness of Garth's good friend, Arthur Mainwaring,[51] who had contributed a prefatory poem in praise of *The Dispensary* and who had taken part in the anti-Blackmorean *Commendatory Verses*. Likewise, in 1715 we find Garth and Blackmore serving together at the deathbed of the earl of Wharton.[52]

Amid his increasing political, social, and professional activities, Garth continued his literary efforts—though he was at best a far from prolific author. As early as 1700, Dr. James Drake had sadly noted the smallness of Garth's poetic production:

> Yes *Garth:* thy Enemies confess thy Store,
> They burst with Envy, yet they long for more:
> Ev'n we, thy Friends, in doubt thy Kindness call,
> To see thy Stock so large, and Gift so small.
> But Jewels in small Cabinets are laid,
> And richest Wines in little Casks convey'd.[53]

Yet, Garth's literary efforts, if not voluminous, at least remained steady. Along with issuing new and revised editions of *The Dispensary* (the fifth in 1703 and the sixth in 1706), in the early years of the new century Garth composed several poems for the theater—a "Prologue to *Tamerlane*" (1701), a "Prologue to *Squire Trelooby*" (1704), and a "Prologue Spoken at the Opening of the Queen's Theatre in the Hay-Market" (1705). To these years also belong such political verses as "On the King of Spain"

(1706) and the verses "To the Earl of Godolphin" on the occasion of his dismissal in 1710 (see chapter 4).

It was only a few months after Garth had offered Godolphin his condolences that Godolphin returned the compliment in "The Earl of Godolphin to Dr. Samuel Garth, Upon the Loss of Miss Dingle: In Return to the Doctor's Consolatory Verses to Him Upon the Loss of His Rod." In this poem Godolphin opens by praising Garth's double talents as a physician and poet ("Thou, happy bard, whose double-gifted pen, / Alike can cure an aching corn, or spleen")[54] and then goes on to devote the bulk of his fifty-three-line verse to expressions of sympathy over Garth's recent "bereavement":

> Dingle is lost, the hollow caves resound,
> Dingle is lost, and multiply the sound;
> Till Echo, chanting it by just degree,
> Shortens to ding, then softens it to D.[55]

For the most part, Garth's biographers have either ignored this enigmatic poem or merely mentioned it in passing without undertaking to explain who the mysterious Miss Dingle might be or what occasioned her "loss" to Garth. An exception is Theodor Schenk, who, in his *Sir Samuel Garth und seine Stellung zum komischen Epos,* praises the "rührenden, teilnehmenden" quality of Godolphin's poem and offers conjectures about its subject: "Wie es scheint, war Miss Dingle ein junges mädchen, vielleicht eine verwandte, die bei Garth wohnte und ihm die wirtschaft führte, wahrscheinlich aber zu ihm noch in näheren beziehungen stand; sie scheint sich selbst das leben genommen zu haben"[56] ("It would appear that Miss Dingle was a young girl, perhaps a relative, who lived with Garth and kept his house or possibly had a closer relationship with him; she seems to have taken her own life"). Schenk is correct in his assumption that "Miss Dingle" was a relative of Garth's, but as a foreign reader he has understandably missed the patently ironic tone of the poem, and thus has failed to realize that it is not the young lady's death (and still less her suicide) that Godolphin is commemorating. Rather, the evidence suggests that "Miss Dingle" was Garth's daughter, and the "loss" referred to is her elopement and marriage in late 1710 or early 1711.

The confusion arises in part from the general dearth of information about Garth's marriage and its issue. We know that

Garth married Martha, daughter of Sir Henry Beaufoy—presumably in the early 1690s, though no record of the wedding date has been found. Moreover, Garth's wife has remained the shadowiest of figures, unmentioned in the letters of Garth's friends and referred to only once in his own surviving correspondence: in an undated note to Sir Hans Sloane, Garth writes: "Be so good to call at my house, Mrs Garth is ill."[57] Beyond such meager scraps, nothing is known of Garth's wife, other than that she died (possibly from the sickness referred to above) on May 1, 1717.[58]

Out of this marriage, according to an anonymous eighteenth-century life of Garth, there came "an only Daughter, who was married to Colonel [William] Boyle, Brother to Henry Boyle, Esq, Speaker of the House of Commons in Ireland, & one of his Majesty's Lord Justices for that Kingdom."[59] To this we may add a letter dating from about 1711, in which Arabelle Pulteney reports the recent marriage of Garth's daughter to "Colonel Boyle," explaining that the couple had eloped. By way of commentary on that elopement, the letter closes with a copy of Godolphin's mock-consolatory verses "On the Loss of Miss Dingle."[60]

Read as a comic offer of sympathy to a friend whose paternal authority has just been challenged by an independent-minded daughter, Godolphin's poem becomes less enigmatic—though not altogether so, since the point of calling Garth's daughter "Miss Dingle" (her name, like her mother's, was Martha) would seem to depend upon a pun or wordplay whose precise meaning has been obscured by time. In the first number of *The Examiner* Garth's verses "To the Earl of Godolphin" had been attacked by Prior, who signed himself "Philodingle," perhaps with ironic reference to the eighteenth-century slang usage of "dingle" in the sense of "hackneyed" or "used up."[61] Though it seems obvious that Godolphin's "Upon the Loss of Miss Dingle" involves a mocking reference to Prior, the exact application of the private joke that lurks behind the name is by now not easily recoverable. How Garth felt about his daughter's elopement is not known, although the bantering tone of Godolphin's poem implies a response of rueful amusement rather than of outrage. If Garth did feel any patriarchal indignation over his daughter's elopement, it did not last; for in his will (written in 1717) he bequeathed his entire estate to her.[62]

V Garth During the Whig Eclipse of 1710-1714

As the eighteenth century entered its second decade, the Whig party, with which Garth had for so long been identified, fell upon hard times. Godolphin's dismissal from office had proved to be the beginning of a general collapse of the Whig ministry under whose direction England had played a dominant role in the War of the Spanish Succession. By 1710 the nation had grown weary of the expensive and seemingly endless war, and accordingly Queen Anne—in response not only to the election returns, but also to her own deepest political sympathies— removed the Whig ministers and appointed a Tory cabinet under the coleadership of Robert Harley (later earl of Oxford) and Henry St. John (later Viscount Bolingbroke). As the triumphant Tories took immediate steps to negotiate England's withdrawal from the war, the Whigs entered a period of disarray from which they were not to emerge for four years. During his party's stay in the political wilderness, Garth (unlike some of his fellow writers) remained unswerving in his loyalties. A letter of Dr. William Stratford of Christ Church offers a glimpse of Garth serving the Whig cause, however humbly, even as the old ministry was toppling. Reporting to the earl of Oxford on September 6, 1710, Stratford writes: "It is said a commission was ordered to make Duke Hamilton Governor of Edinburgh Castle, that upon this news the Duke of Argyll had written a very angry letter—it is not said to whom—threatening the utmost revenge, if that place were so disposed of. That at the same time he had sent a copy of his letter to several friends, desiring them to publish it in all coffee houses, that amongst others a copy was sent to Dr. Garth, who had gone round all the coffee houses to read it."[63] A month later, in October, 1710, Garth was asked to serve as editor of the newly-founded Whig *Medley*.[64] Though Garth did not accept the job, he did join Addison, Steele, and other prominent Whig literati as a contributor.[65]

To Garth, an especially distressing aspect of this period was the Tory campaign to discredit the duke of Marlborough. Because of Marlborough's popularity as a victorious general, the Tories thought it would be impolitic to remove him summarily. Instead, he was retained as commander (though under orders to initiate no battles), while at home the Tory press—at first tentatively, but then with increasing boldness—disparaged his character and even his generalship. In mid-1711 Garth traveled to the Continent, his major purpose being to deliver messages to Marlborough from the Whig forces in England. In July, 1711, Henry Watkins, who had no high opinion of Garth's political discretion, wrote to John Drummond:

I told you in my last Dr. Garth was arrived here [i.e., Marlborough's continental headquarters], and now tell you he intends to go away tomorrow. I cannot find he has been very lavish with his tongue but dare venture to assure you, my Lord Duke has trusted him with nothing but what may be safely proclaimed at Charing Cross. I dined with his Grace the day after the doctor's arrival, and he told us very merrily of the letters the doctor brought him from Lady Duchess, Lord Godolphin, and Mr. Craggs. He said that by the colour and smell of them it would seem as if the doctor had made use of no other paper on any occasion during the whole voyage. You may believe he will have answers to the letters he brought, but they will be such as need not be whispered, and if he had anything to tell, you will not have your share of it, for he intends to go home by Ostend.[66]

A second reference to Garth's visit on this occasion occurs in a letter by General Hans Hamilton, who wrote to the earl of Oxford that "Dr. Garth made a short visit here of three days; the morning after his arrival he was locked up about two hours with 73 [the code reference to Marlborough] when no one else had admittance; he would willingly have stayed to see tomorrow's march, but was hastened away, and for more expedition goes to Ostend."[67]

In December, 1711, the Tories finally moved decisively against the duke, dismissing him from his command and charging him with profiteering in army contracts. Marlborough returned to England, where the Whigs rallied to his defense; but by the end of 1712 the duke and his wife had found the political climate at home so uncongenial that they decided to move back to the Continent and live in "exile." It was on their departure that Garth received from the duchess the diamond ring mentioned earlier. Surprisingly, Garth's only known poetic commemoration of the duke's dismissal and expatriation consists of a passing reference in "On Her Majesty's Statue" (1715) and a few allusions added to the eighth edition (1718) of *The Dispensary.*

During the years of the Tory ascendancy Garth's major literary concern was a proposed Latin edition of the works of ing their hold on office, the Peace of Utrecht seemed to complete the repudiation of the Godolphin ministry. Garth commemorated the signing of the peace with a dinner party whose funereal quality is apparent in the report of Bishop Berkeley. Writing to Sir John Perceval on May 2, 1713, Berkeley says: "The very day on which the peace was proclaimed, instead of associating with Tories, I dined with several of the other party at Dr. Garth's, where we drank the Duke of Marlborough's health, though they had not the heart to speak one word against the peace, and indeed the spirit of the Whigs seems quite broken, and is not likely to recover."[74]

VI *Later Career*

Despite Berkeley's gloomy view of Whig prospects, the Tory ministry lasted only a little more than a year after the Peace of Utrecht. In August, 1714, Queen Anne suddenly died, and with the accession of George I, the Whigs were triumphantly returned to office. As a reward for his loyal service, Garth received the first knighthood conferred by the new monarch. Of the ceremony, we are told that Garth "asked as a special favour that the accolade might be given him with Marlborough's sword, and the King complied with this in much good humour."[75] Further signs of royal appreciation came early in 1715 when Garth was appointed both physician-in-ordinary to the king and physician-general to the army.

With the restoration of his party to office, Garth's political activities increased. The records we have are spotty, but they suggest that in the four years remaining to him, Garth served the Whig cause as a combination of unofficial spokesman, private emissary, and gatherer of political intelligence. It is in some such capacity that we find him traveling in the north of England during the Jacobite Revolt of 1715, when he writes to his fellow Kit-Cat, the duke of Newcastle:

I find the ordinary people are pretty well inclin'd in ye Bishop-rick of Durham, and that ye thoughts of ye invasion has brought them to some reason. I have taken care in all places to give them a right impression of ye King and Government. I shall next Thursday turn my face towards where my heart is and hope to Kiss yor hand in ten days. I shall not goe into Scotland I think till an Earthquake heavs mee thither. I wonder that ye Devil who can bee where hee pleases, shoud at present take a fancy to bee so mutch there. Wee have not here any man-ner of account of ye Scotch Camp, which makes mee conclude wee need not bee in great anxiety about ye event of that affair.[76]

At the time this letter was sent to him, Thomas Pelham-Holles, duke of Newcastle and earl of Clare, was just beginning his long career in Whig politics. He had been helpful in getting Garth appointed as physician-in-ordinary to the king,[77] and after 1714 he became close to Garth as a friend, patron, patient, and sometime recipient of political soundings like the above. Something of the nature of their relationship (as well as Garth's skill as a courtier) can be seen in another of his letters to Newcastle: "At my coming down to town I found a hundred Guinnys in ye purse you gave mee . . . tho' I can never over value ye least friendship of yours, you are resolv'd to over value ye greatest service of mine. I wou'd gladly have you oblig'd to me, but yor generosity makes it impossible. I hope ye Dutchess of Newcastle is quite well. tis strange she shou'd be so ill treated by ye ayr of ye Sea from whence she rose. a Poet thinks it no more reasonable for ye daughter of Jupiter to be a Goddess than ye Grandaughters of Mars [the Duchess was a granddaughter of the Duke of Marlborough]."[78] It was in honor of Newcastle's country home in Surrey that Garth, in April, 1715, published his most ambitious and considerable poem since *The Dispensary*— *Claremont*, a "place" poem in the tradition of Denham's *Cooper's Hill* and Pope's *Windsor Forest* (see chapter 4).

In mid-1715, shortly after the publication of *Claremont*, Garth embarked upon a European trip that lasted until late in the following year. Pope, in a letter to Martha Blount (July 23, 1715) mentions Italy as Garth's destination.[79] There is no reason to believe that Garth's Italian visit was anything other than a pleasure trip; on his return journey, however, he stopped in Paris for a delicate political mission as informal emissary to the deposed Tory minister, Bolingbroke. Bolingbroke had fled to France to escape prosecution after the new Whig ministry had accused him of having carried on treasonous negotiations with the Pretender. On first arriving in France Bolingbroke had joined the Jacobites, even briefly serving as secretary of state in James III's court in exile. By late 1716, however, Bolingbroke had been dismissed from that job, and there were some among the

Whigs who thought he might be receptive to proselytizers from their party. It was in furtherance of this potentially valuable conversion that Garth dallied in Paris during the fall of 1716.

Garth and Bolingbroke had been on friendly terms since at least 1701, when Bolingbroke (then Henry St. John) praised Garth in *A Pindarick Ode* for his "living Verse and healing Arts."[80] Bolingbroke's confidence in those "healing Arts" had even led him to become Garth's patient, as we see in a letter of October 2, 1705, in which Bolingbroke speaks of going to the country for a few days "by Dr. Garth's direction."[81] Garth, for his part, reciprocated Bolingbroke's esteem, and since neither man had allowed subsequent political differences to estrange him from the other, Garth was well-qualified to help sound out Bolingbroke's mood in exile.

Unfortunately, neither Garth nor Bolingbroke left an account of their conversations, but there is ample evidence of the concern those meetings inspired among the Jacobites. Writing to the duke of Mar from Paris in August, 1716, John Menzies at first simply reports the presence of "Garth and some assistants"[82] — most notably Addison and Craggs. A month later, on September 24, Lewis Inese writes Mar in some alarm at the Whig overtures to Bolingbroke: "I am told by two persons that Boynton [the code name for Bolingbroke] has had private meetings lately with some of Williamson's family [the Whigs]. We have here of that gang Craggs, Garth, Addison and other smart men, but I know not who it was that saw Boynton."[83] A few days later, on September 29, Inese reports: "It is no more to be doubted that Boynton has of late had several private meetings and suppers with the chief persons of Williamson's family here, especially with Dr. Garth, who is now returned to England, and Mr. Craggs, both Mildmay's [i.e., Marlborough's] creatures."[84] Shortly thereafter, Menzies writes Mar of his fear that the Whig efforts to win over Bolingbroke might succeed, and he quotes Garth as having said that Bolingbroke was "one of the best subjects K[ing] Geo[rge] has. He found him so."[85] For all of Menzies's fear, Bolingbroke did not succumb to the Whig blandishments, though he continued to feel warmly toward Garth, affectionately characterizing him as "the best natured ingenious wild man I ever knew."[86]

Soon after his return to England, Garth was the recipient of an anonymous hortatory poem (printed for Bernard Lintot) called

An Espistle to Sir Samuel Garth, Occasion'd by the Landing of the Pretender, and the Report of His Royal Highness the Prince of Wales's Going to Scotland (1716). After celebrating Garth's prowess as a poet and champion of the Hanoverian succession, the author urges him to join his fellow authors in standing up for the king in the current crisis:

> Congreve for this the Lyre neglected strings,
> In Addison a second Virgil sings.
> Nor wilt thou, Garth, unmindful of the Day,
> Refuse to Britain's Hopes a Solemn Lay:
> Not Unrewarded will descend the Song,
> That must, with Theirs, the Poet's Fame prolong.
> To Bless, like them is First: the Next Degree
> Of Mortal Glory is to Praise like Thee.[87]

Garth, who needed little prompting in this cause, responded later that year with his poem "On the New Conspiracy, 1716."

The most imposing literary effort of Garth's latter years came to fruition with the publication in July, 1717, of his English edition of Ovid's *Metamorphoses*. Among the eighteen translators were some of the most distinguished writers of the day, including Dryden, Addison, Gay, Congreve, Pope, and Rowe. Garth himself, in addition to his editor's preface, contributed the translation of Book 14 and the tale of Cippus in book 15. Sumptuously printed by Tonson, Garth's Ovid was immediately popular, and it subsequently became the eighteenth century's most reprinted English translation of the *Metamorphoses* (see chapter 4).

After the publication of his Ovid edition, Garth turned again to travel and renewed political activity. Despite his growing poor health, the spring of 1718 found him again in France, where he revisited Bolingbroke and contemplated another trip to Italy. Writing to Newcastle from Paris, Garth reports:

I have been very much indispos'd since I came hither, but I shall have this advantage from it, I shall have ye pleasure of seeing yor Grace sooner. if I should goe to Rome it woud be a reall Pilgramage for I can neither eat nor sleep, and therefor think of being in England in less than a month. ye Ld Bolingbroke is at Aix la Chapell with Mad^m Vallet [the marquise de Villette, whom Bolingbroke married in 1720] a Lady with whom he has an Intimacy as they say here. . . . ye Ld Stayrs [John

Dalrymple, earl of Stair—the British ambassador] kept ye Birth day [of George I—May 28] with great Pomp, and worthy ye happy occasion. his Lady presented me with a very fine sword to vindicate ye Title of our brave and good King, if any of ye Jacobites shoud dare to question it. I can assure you our Ambassador lives magnificently and may be admir'd by ye foreign ministers, but not imitated. ye Evning of ye Birthday my great prudence prevented three young Gentlemen of Quality from leaping into a great Bason in ye publick walks in ye Tuleries, but I was against ye Frolick because it was not filld with Champagn, as They were.[88]

Garth evidently remained in Paris longer than the month he anticipated, for on June 20, 1718, we find Sir Thomas Higgons reporting on Garth's visit in a letter to the duke of Mar: "Very few of our countrymen are at Paris at present. Dr. Garth is there, whom my brother saw. He speaks with respect of his master George, but says the Prince, his son, is such a scoundrel that he is despised by everybody, and has very few partisans, and that he will never be able to hold the reins; if he should ever come to govern."[89] There is no way of knowing if Higgons is accurate in his paraphrase of Garth's opinion, though we may question whether Garth would really choose such a time and place to be quite so outspoken about a prince whom he had in 1711 described as "the Happiness and Expectation of *Europe.*"[90]

VII Garth's Death: "... a Good Christian, Without Knowing Himself to be so"

As he had forseen in his letter to Newcastle, Garth's worsening health prevented him from going on to Italy, and by the late summer or early fall of 1718 he was back in England. There is no record of the nature of his illness, but its effects were soon obvious enough to alarm his friends. In "To my Friend Dr. *Garth* In his Sickness," George Granville (Lord Lansdowne) urges the "*God of* Poetry *and* Physick," Appollo:

> Sire of all Arts, defend thy darling Son;
> O! save the Man whose life's so much our own!
> On whom, like *Atlas,* the whole World's reclin'd,
> And by restoring *Garth,* preserve Mankind.[91]

Garth was a good enough physician to recognize the seriousness of his own condition, and once the unlikelihood of recovery became apparent, he seems to have found the prospect of a lingering illness more depressing than the advent of death itself. Such, at any rate, is the import of a footnote appended to an anonymous poem "Occasion'd by the Death of Dr. Garth": "The Doctor being ask'd in his Sickness how he did? Answer'd, I long till this Ceremony of Death is over."[92] To this we may add the remark of John Barber, in a letter to Swift on April 22, 1735: "You may remember Dr. *Garth* said he was glad when he was dying; for he was weary of having his shoes pulled off and on."[93]

If we can believe one contemporary account, Garth's impatience at the tardiness of death may have led him to take steps toward hastening its progress. In Spence's *Anecdotes,* we are told that one of Garth's personal friends—identified only as a "Mr. Townley, of Townley in Lancashire"—told the following story of his last illness:

When Dr. Garth had been for a good while in a bad state of health, he sent one day for a physician with whom he was particularly intimate, and conjured him by their friendship and by everything that was more sacred (if there was anything more sacred) to tell him sincerely whether he thought he should ever be able to get rid of his illness or not. His friend, thus conjured, told him that "he thought he might struggle on with it perhaps for some years, but that he much feared he could never get the better of it entirely." Dr. Garth thanked him for his dealing so fairly with him, turned the discourse to other things, and talked very cheerfully all the rest of the time he stayed with him.

As soon as he was gone, he called for his servant, said he was a good deal out of order and would go to bed, and then sent him for a surgeon to bleed him. Soon after, he sent for a second surgeon by a different servant, and was bled in the other arm. He then said he wanted rest, and when everybody had quitted the room he took off the bandages and lay down with a design of bleeding to death. . . . He afterwards sunk into a sound sleep, slept all the night, waked in the morning without his usual pains, and said that "if it would continue so, he could be content to live on." In his last illness he did not use any remedies, but let his distemper take its course.—The former I have had more than once from his own mouth.[94]

This alleged suicide attempt is not confirmed by any other source, though Garth's avoidance of medication prior to his death is mentioned by Pope, whom Spence quotes as saying: "[Garth] did not take any care of himself in his last illness, and had talked for three or four years as one tired of living. In short, I believe he was willing *to let it go.*"⁹⁵

The final crisis came in January, 1719, when *The Original Weekly Journal* (January 17), *The Weekly Packet* (January 10-17), and *The Weekly Medley* (January 10-17) all carried notices of Garth's worsening condition, the latter journal reporting that "On Wednesday Night (Jan. 14) Sir Samuel Garth was given over by his Physicians." Death came on Sunday morning, January 18, and on Thursday, January 22, Garth was buried in St. Mary's Church of Harrow-on-the-Hill in a vault beside his wife, Martha, whose death had come two years earlier. In its obituary notice, *The Original Weekly Journal* (January 24) characterized Garth as "one of the most celebrated Physicians of the Age. He is universally regreted, being a Gentleman of extraordinary Charity."

Not everyone was prepared to be so generous to Garth's memory, however, and within a few days of his death there began to circulate stories claiming that he had gone to his grave as a professed and impenitent atheist. Such charges of irreligion against Garth were hardly new, for throughout his career his enemies had accused him of impiety. It will be recalled, for example, how he was criticized for his supposedly "pagan" oration at Dryden's funeral; and the author of *The St. Alban's Ghost* (cited above) found Garth's Christianity as spurious as his poetry. In a similar vein, Arbuthnot, in *Notes and Memorandums of the Six Days preceding the Death of a Late Right Reverend,* pictures Garth as telling a dying clergyman who seeks religious solace: "Why, Sir, have you the vanity to think that religion ever did our cause any service! If that comes into your head, and you squeak at last, it is time for me to bid you good night.... I'll tell the Kit-Cat Club of you, and it shall be known to every man at C[our]t that you die like a pedant." ⁹⁶ Such charges were, of course, common coin in the polemics of the day, and by themselves they would constitute very poor evidence as to Garth's actual religious feelings. Upon Garth's death, however, there were a number of new reports—not all of them from his enemies—tending to confirm the view that Garth, if not the mocking blasphemer his disparagers made him out to be, was at least something less than a model of conventional piety.

In the week following Garth's demise, *The Weekly Journal or Saturday's-Post* (January 24, 1719) cryptically told its readers:

" 'Tis said that Sir Samuel Garth, a Day or two before he died, sent an extraordinary sort of a Message to an eminent Poet in Surrey-Street in the Strand, and though the same has been well attested by several Persons of Honour and Quality, we have thought fit for sundry Reasons not to publish it." The "eminent Poet in Surrey-Street" was Congreve, himself seriously ill at the time, and the nature of the message is revealed in the manuscripts of the earl of Egmont, who writes: "When dying, [Garth] sent to Congreve to let him know he was going [on] his Journey, and desired to know how soon he would follow him. Congreve sent him back word, that he wish'd him a good journey, but did not intend to take the same road."[97]

Somewhat analogous is the story of a final exchange between Garth and Addison. Spence, citing Edward Young as his source, tells us only that "Garth sent to Addison (of whom he had a very high opinion) when on his death-bed, to tell him whether the Christian religion was true."[98] Presumably, this is the occasion referred to in Berkeley's *The Analyst* (1734), where he writes that "[Addison] assured me that the infidelity of a certain noted mathematician, still living, was one principal reason assigned by a witty man of those times for his being an infidel."[99] Berkeley does not identify the "mathematician" or the "witty man," but Joseph Stock, who probably consulted Berkeley's brother on this matter, writes:

The occasion [of *The Analyst*] was this: Mr. Addison had given the bishop an account of their common friend Dr. Garth's behaviour in his last illness, which was equally unpleasing to both those excellent advocates for revealed religion. For when Mr. Addison went to see the doctor, and began to discourse with him seriously about preparing for his approaching dissolution, the other made answer, "Surely, Addison, I have good reason not to believe those trifles, since my friend Dr. [Edmund] Halley who has dealt so much in demonstration has assured me that the doctrines of Christianity are incomprehensible, and the religion itself an imposture."[100]

Another reference to Garth's dismissal of religion in his last days comes from the diary of Thomas Hearne, who was one of those who thought Garth's oration for Dryden impious. In his entry for July 24, 1724, Hearne remarks: "I am told Dr. Garth, who writ that famous English Poem called *The Dispensary*, was a Man of no Religion, that when he was upon his Death-bed and the Subject of another Life mentioned to him, he said, he had done what good he could, and he did not trouble himself about what was to come."[101]

It was in response to stories like these that Pope rose up to defend his old friend. As early as 1715 Pope had described Garth, in "A Farewell to London," as "the best good Christian he, / Altho' he knows it not."[102] After Garth's death, in a letter (ca. 1720) to Charles Jervas, Pope echoes that earlier description: "After these [i.e., other recently dead friends], the best natur'd of Men, Sir *Samuel Garth,* has left me in the truest concern for his loss. His death was very Heroical, and yet unaffected enough to have made a Saint, or a Philosopher famous: but ill Tongues, and worse Hearts have branded even his last Moments, as wrongfully as they did his Life, with irreligion. You must have heard many Tales on this Subject; but if ever there was a good Christian, without knowing himself to be so, it was Dr. *Garth."*[103]

Even more at odds with the prevailing accounts of Garth's final sentiments on religion—not to mention the story of his attempted suicide—are two further references, both attributed to Pope, in which the dying Garth, far from spurning Christianity, formally embraces Roman Catholicism. In the first of these (which are both in Spence's *Anecdotes),* Pope is quoted as saying that "Garth talked in a less libertine manner . . . the last three years of his life. He was rather doubtful and fearful than religious. It was usual for him to say that 'if there was any such thing as religion, 'twas among the Roman Catholics.' "[104] In the second, less equivocal allusion, Spence reports Pope as flatly asserting: "[Garth] died a Papist (as I was assured by Mr. [Edward] Blount, who carried the father to him in his last hours), probably from the greater efficacy we give the sacraments."[105] Beyond these two references in Spence, there is no other authority for this conversion, which appears all the more dubious in light of Pope's failure to mention it in his letter to Jervas.

To a modern reader, neither Garth, the blaspheming atheist, nor Garth, the last minute convert, seems altogether convincing. In his works and letters, Garth's references to Christianity, while few in number, are neither mocking nor antagonistic, although at least one present-day critic detects a "deistic" tenor in the preface to the *Metamorphoses.*[106] In general, the preponderance of the more reliable evidence suggests that Garth—while often wittily irreverent in conversation—was not so much hostile to revealed religion as he was disinclined, even in the face of death, to seek its comforts. To some of his contemporaries, indifference to the claims of religion at such a time no doubt seemed tantamount to open defiance. At this late date, however, we can only guess as to Garth's deeper feelings about religion. Perhaps the one formulation that may be confidently endorsed is that ascribed to Garth himself in a traditional anecdote, which has him replying to an inquiry about his creed: " 'That he was of the religion of wise men.' Being asked to explain himself, he remarked, 'That wise men kept their own secrets.' "[107]

VIII   "The Best-Natured Man"

However much they might decry his presumed religious attitudes, when it came to Garth's character as a physician few of his contemporaries had anything but praise.[108] Garth's high professional reputation is reflected not only in the honors and offices he achieved, but in the frequent testimonials that came from his friends and patients. Of such endorsements (some of which have been quoted earlier), one of the most graceful was written by Steele, who dedicated *The Lover* (1714) to Garth. In that dedication Steele praises Garth's abilities as a physician and extols the generosity with which they are exercised: "The Manner in which You practise this heavenly Faculty of aiding human Life, is according to the Liberality of Science, and demonstrates that your Heart is more set upon doing Good than growing Rich. The pitiful Artifices which Empyricks are guilty of to drain Cash out of Valetudinarians, are the Abhorrence of your generous Mind; and it is as common with *Garth* to supply indigent Patients with Money for Food, as to receive it from Wealthy ones for Physick."[109]

In commending Garth for his charity as a physician, Steele echoes the opinion of many others, such as Thomas Killigrew (". . . no unhappy Person ever apply'd to him, but that he made use of the utmost of his Interest to ease their Pain and Anxiety"),[110] Giles Jacob ("He was an Excellent Physician, Affable and Courteous in his Behaviour, and never better pleased than in doing good Offices, either to Friends or Strangers, who required his Assistance"),[111] and Joseph Warton

("It was said of [Garth], that 'No Physician knew his Art more, nor his Trade less' ").[112] To his obituarist in *The Weekly Packet* (January 17-24, 1719) the modest size of Garth's estate was convincing evidence of how well he had practiced the medical charity he preached in *The Dispensary;* since "considering the Esteem he was in, and the Opportunities he had, it is obvious he might have made himself wealthy, had he not made many others happy. Many of his Profession have grown rich by receiving fewer Fees than Sir Samuel refus'd."

Beyond the general praise for his professional skills and generosity, some scattered evidence has come down to us concerning Garth's bedside manner, which seems to have been direct, informal, and sometimes brisk to the point of abruptness. Thus, one of his notes to Sir Hans Sloane shows not only Garth's benevolence, but his laconic forthrightness: "Dear S^r[:] If you can recommend this miserable Slut to be flux'd you'll doe an action of Charity. I am S^r Yo^r most obedient Servant[,] S. Garth."[113] It was presumably Garth's reputation for such bluntness with patients that led Arbuthnot to satirize his sickroom deportment. In *The History of John Bull* (1712) Garth is shown in attendance upon an ailing "old woman"—i.e., the Church of England—of whom he reports: "In no manner of danger, I vow to Gad, quoth Garth, the old woman is hysterical, fanciful, Sir, I vow to Gad. . . ."[114] Elsewhere Arbuthnot parodies Garth's cavalier manner as seen through the eyes of an anxious patient: "Hear G[art]h coming up stairs: now for my last sentence: how shall I receive it? What shall I say to him? Order my servant to give ten pieces: that may soften him perhaps. He comes in singing: looks with a bad aspect: recommends an undertaker to me. Sighs often. The doctor smiles; bows, and says, no good can be done! sad words!"[115] In a similar vein is the anecdote which has Garth replying (when reminded that he has forgotten to visit his patients that day): "It's no great matter whether I see them to-night, or not, for nine of them have such bad constitutions that all the physicians in the world can't save them; and the other six have such good constitutions that all the physicians in the world can't kill them."[116]

It was not Garth's bedside manner as much as his ballroom manner that on one occasion led the duchess of Marlborough to question his medical judgment. On May 28, 1716, the duke of Marlborough suffered a stroke and, on Garth's recommendation, went to Bath to recuperate. The duchess, writing to Craggs, questioned Garth's faith in the curative powers of the waters at Bath, adding: "I think Sr S: Garth is the most honest & compassionate, but after the minuets which I have seen him dance and his late tour into Italy, I can't help thinking that hee may some times bee in the wrong."[117]

Another of Garth's illustrious patients has left conflicting testimony as to his professional demeanor. In 1713, Lady Mary Wortley Montagu's brother, William Pierrepont (earl of Kingston), fell sick, and Garth, who was the family physician, was called in. Writing to her husband on June 25, Lady Mary reports: "My Brother, they send me word, is as well as can be expected. But Dr. Garth says 'tis the worst sort, . . . which I should think very forbodeing if I did not know all Doctors (and particularly Garth) love to have their Patients in Danger."[118] Since Pierrepont died of this illness, Garth's pessimism would seem to have been justified. A year and a half later, however, Garth treated Lady Mary for smallpox, and this time she found his prognosis overly optimistic, rather than the reverse. In the rueful poem she wrote upon her recovery, "Saturday, or the Small-Pox," Garth appears as "Machaon" (Greek physician at the siege of Troy):

> MACHAON too, the great MACHAON, known
> By his red cloak and his superior frown;
> And why, he cry'd, this grief and this despair?
> You shall be well, again be fair;
> Believe my oath; (with that an oath he swore)
> False was his oath; my beauty is no more![119]

Despite Lady Mary's ironic description of Garth's "superior frown," his habitual expression seems to have been jovial rather than dour. Abel Boyer says of Garth's appearance, "his Looks is smiling and cheerful";[120] John Lacy speaks of how ". . . G[ar]th, of Butler's mending Race, / Wears the Paternal Comick on his Face";[121] and Daniel Kenrick remarks of Garth, "cheerful [was] his Look and manly . . . his Mien."[122] The best known likeness of Garth was done by Godfrey Kneller as part of a series of Kit-Cat portraits. In it we find Garth neither smiling nor frowning, but rather wearing an expression of calm, portly dignity. His willingness to put aside that dignity emerges in an amusing incident that has some bearing on his physique, if not his face. Again the source is Lady Mary Wortley Montagu, who writes to Frances Hewet in October, 1709, that "There is another story that I had from a hand I dare depend upon. The Duke of Grafton [Charles Fitzroy] and Dr. Garth ran a foot-match in the Mall of 200 yards, and the latter, to his immortal glory, beat."[123] The comedy of this athletic contest lay in the fact that both participants were notably fat.

In his aforementioned dedication of *The Lover* to Garth, Steele writes: "As soon as I thought of making the *Lover* a Present to one of my Friends, I resolved, without farther distracting my Choice, to send it *To the Best-natured Man*. You are so universally known for this Character, that an Epistle so directed would find its Way to You without your Name, and I believe no Body but You yourself would deliver such a Superscription to any other Person."[124] Dedications are not noted for their objectivity, but beneath the hyperbole, Steele was simply endorsing an opinion that nearly all of Garth's friends voiced at one time or another. As we have seen, terms such as "good-natured," "best-natured," and "most amiable" run like a leit-motif through the comments made by Pope, Addison, Bolingbroke, and the many others who recorded their impressions of Garth's character. Even the mysterious "Mr. Townley," who told Spence of Garth's alleged suicide attempt, added "that the Doctor was the most agreeable companion he ever knew."[125]

The same good nature that made Garth so charitable in his medical practice was equally manifest in his general willingness to use his influence with powerful friends for the benefit of others. "As his own Merit procur'd him a great Interest with those in power," wrote one eighteenth-century biographer, "so his Humanity & good Nature inclin'd him to make use of that Interest, rather for the Support & Encouragement of other Men of Learning & Genius, than for the Advancement of his own Fortune."[126] More emphatic yet is *The Weekly Packet* (January 17–24, 1719), which reported that "It is said of him, that he never did an ill-natur'd Thing to any Person, nor ever refus'd a good One, when it lay within his Power: He has, on the contrary, done numberless Acts of Benevolence and Liberality, that were unsought, and even shunn'd." Though common sense suggests that Garth was probably not quite the implausible paragon his panegyrists make him out to be, his surviving correspondence amply confirms his lifelong habit of generosity toward others. Of

Life of Garth

the thirty-one Garth letters that have survived, no fewer than twelve are devoted entirely or in large part to solicitations in behalf of one or another needy petitioner.[127] It seems altogether fitting that Sir Samuel Garth, whose private benevolence as a doctor and as a man so endeared him to his friends, should have earned his wider, literary fame as an eloquent apostle of public charity in an age not noted for its social compassion.

CHAPTER 2

The Dispensary: *The Historical and Literary Background*

I *Bellum Medicinale*

ON September 23, 1518, King Henry VIII—distressed by "the audacity of those wicked men who . . . profess medicine more for the sake of their avarice than from the assurance of any good conscience"—proclaimed the establishment of "a perpetual College of learned and grave men" who would henceforth enjoy exclusive rights for the practice of medicine "in our City of London and the suburbs, and within seven miles from that City on every side."[1] To ensure high standards, the charter of the Royal College of Physicians of London limited membership to thirty fellows and specified that these could be selected only from recipients of Oxford or Cambridge medical degrees. Thus launched, the College of Physicians went on to flourish, as subsequent monarchs and charter revisions reaffirmed its authority and gradually widened its functions to include, among other things, the regulation of such lesser figures in the medical hierarchy as midwives, barber-surgeons, and apothecaries.

For the first century of its existence, the professional supremacy of the College of Physicians was scarcely questioned. Nor did there seem at first any threat to that supremacy when in 1617 another royal charter established the Society of the Art and Mystery of Apothecaries of London, thus giving new prominence and definition to a group which had hitherto been submerged in the Grocers Company. The charter of the apothecaries' society, while granting its members a monopoly on the preparation and sale of drugs in London and its environs, made clear that this privilege was not to be exercised "to the prejudice of the President and College or Commonality of the Physicians of the City of *London,* nor to take away, break, or make void, the

Jurisdiction, Authority, Oversight, or Correction of the said President and College. . . ."[2] Moreover, the subsidiary position of the apothecaries was emphasized by provisions requiring the society to consult with the college prior to adopting any new drug regulations or accepting new applicants for membership. Lastly, in a provision which was to generate much resentment, the monopoly earlier granted to apothecaries was qualified to allow physicians the right to compound and sell their own prescriptions if they so desired.

As the seventeenth century progressed, the apothecaries showed signs of increasing restiveness over their inferior status and the general tendency of physicians to treat pharmacists as unskilled tradesmen, rather than as professional colleagues. In large measure, the physicians' attitude found its justification in the obvious and considerable discrepancy in education between the two groups. Physicians, beyond receiving the classical university education of the day, had to spend several additional years mastering the works of ancient and modern medical authorities. Apothecaries, on the other hand, learned their craft not through formal schooling, but during seven years of adolescent apprenticeship, which (as most doctors saw it) trained them more fully as shopkeepers than as pharmacists. However, it was more than differences of education that separated the two groups; for inextricably tied up with those differences was a powerful class antagonism. Unlike the apothecaries, whose social origins and economic status were mostly humble, the men who comprised the College of Physicians came largely from the upper middle class. Considering themselves as gentlemen, with all that the term implied in the seventeenth century, most doctors were as little impressed by the average apothecary's genealogy as by his medical expertise. In the face of such attitudes, the apothecaries, naturally, were not silent. With considerable logic, they argued that their training, if not always elegant, was nevertheless of a much more practical and useful sort than the largely theoretical medicine taught in the schools. As for the social superiority of doctors, the apothecaries charged that many physicians had become so self-important that they disdained to treat the poor, who perforce had come to depend upon apothecaries for medical treatment.

It was this latter point—the growing numbers of apothecaries who had begun to prescribe medicines, as well as selling them—

that most concerned the doctors. The first serious encroachments of this sort developed during the social and political upheavals attendant upon the Civil War and its aftermath. In that conflict, the political loyalties of most members of the College of Physicians lay with the Royalists: when the court abandoned London for Oxford, some members (like Harvey) went with it, and four years later, when the king fled to France, a few physicians even followed him into exile.[3] Reduced in numbers and without the authority of its royal patron, the college fell on hard times during the Commonwealth. Although the apothecaries also suffered from the disruptions of the war, after the victory of the parliamentary forces (with whom most members sympathized) the society enjoyed a period of expansion and increased activity.[4] Given the diminished condition of the College of Physicians during the Commonwealth, the London apothecaries became bolder than ever in assuming the practice of medicine. Under the circumstances, the College of Physicians could only bide its time and limit its response to such muted indignation as that expressed in the college *Annals* for April 9, 1655: "There was a discussion concerning the restraint of the daring practices of apothecaries . . . But since that former might be pressed with not inconsiderable difficulties . . . it seemed proper for the present to refrain. . . ."[5]

With the Restoration in 1660, the College of Physicians felt better able to reassert its authority, especially after 1663, when Charles II granted the college a new charter with enhanced powers of regulation over apothecaries. But before those powers could be successfully applied, the city was struck by the Great Plague of 1665, which led to a vast increase in the number of apothecaries actively practicing medicine. For so enormous a catastrophe as the plague, the handful of licensed physicians in London would have been woefully inadequate even if they had all remained functioning in the city.[6] In fact, however, as the pestilence spread, many doctors were themselves stricken, and beyond this, a considerable number seem to have fled the city. In later pamphlet exchanges, the apothecaries were to score tellingly with the charge that the cowardly physicians had simply abandoned the sick, whose treatment was thereupon taken up by the dedicated apothecaries. To this damaging indictment, the physicians could only reply that they had left London "not so much for their own Preservation, as [for] the

Service of those whom they attend."[7] This contention was no doubt valid enough, since the king, the court, and almost all of those wealthy enough to consult a doctor had indeed fled the city; but in offering such a defense, the physicians were tacitly conceding that most of the populace, even in normal times, could not afford the services of a licensed practitioner.

By way of counterattack, the physicians charged that during the plague, the apothecaries—far from selflessly attending the afflicted—had callously used the crisis as a chance to line their own pockets at the expense of the desperately sick. Thus, Dr. Nathaniel Hodges (a candidate for the College of Physicians who *had* stayed in London during the plague) charged that: "nothing more contributed [to the death rate] than the Practice of Chymists and Quacks, of whose Audacity and Ignorance it is impossible to be altogether silent; they were indefatigable in spreading their Antidotes; and although equal Strangers to all Learning as well as Physick, they thrust into every Hand some Trash or other under the Disguise of a pompous Title.... Their Medicines were more fatal than the Plague, and added to the Numbers of the Dead."[8]

The bickering between physician and apothecary reached a new level of intensity with the appearance in 1669-1671 of a series of reciprocal polemics. The physicians opened the attack with the publication of Daniel Coxe's *A Discourse, Wherein the Interest of the Patient in Reference to Physick and Physicians is Soberly Debated* (1669). Coxe's comparatively restrained tract was soon followed by a more vehement denunciation of apothecaries, Christopher Merrett's *A Short View of the Frauds and Abuses Committed by Apothecaries* (1670). In this work Merrett indignantly rehearses the familiar charges: apothecaries, though "illiterate" and incompetent outside their narrow trade, are brazenly (and murderously) practicing medicine among the ignorant and credulous. Even when they limit themselves to pharmacy, says Merrett, the apothecaries shamelessly impose upon the public with falsified prescriptions, skimped ingredients, and inflated prices. Merrett's solution was that henceforth all physicians should compound and sell their own drugs, a practice which would effectually render apothecaries superfluous. To the distress of the apothecaries, who saw their very livelihoods thus challenged, Merrett's proposal was quickly endorsed by other physicians, such as Jonathan Goddard, in his *A Discourse Setting Forth the Unhappy Conditions of the Practice of Physick in London* (1670), and Everard Maynwaring, who, in *Praxis Medicorum Antiqua & Nova* (1671), cited the authority of the ancients in support of his contention "That the preparation of Medicines is the proper and special business of every Physician."[9]

The members of the Society of Apothecaries, alarmed at the onslaught and the direction it had taken, responded collectively with a petition of protest to the College of Physicians and individually with a number of pamphlets. In *Lex Talionis; sive Vindiciae Pharmacoporum: Or A Short Reply to Dr. Merrett's Book; and Others, written against the Apothecaries* (1670), the anonymous author contends that a knowledgeable apothecary is more likely to be skillful in treating the sick than a doctor is in compounding medicines. Since the physicians fled London during the plague and have consistently shown themselves too money-hungry to visit the poor, the author thinks the patient should be allowed his own choice of what help to seek: for "good Mr. *Doctor*, . . . if the Patient desire the Visits of the *Apothecary* his Friend, having withall some Confidence of his Parts and Abilities, I hope you have no reason to be angry, but give him his freedom in this."[10] Also taking up the attack is the author of *Medice Cura Teipsum! Or the Apothecaries Plea* (1671), who describes himself on the title page as a "well-wisher" to both sides in the dispute, but who soon makes clear his loyalty to the apothecaries's cause. This author concedes that the apothecaries have in recent years overstepped their prerogatives, but only, he maintains, in order to fill the medical vacuum which physicians had allowed to develop. He upbraids the college for its lack of public spirit, emphatically rejects Merrett's call for doctors to mix their own drugs, and in closing calls upon both sides to respect each other's professional competence.

II "A Repositorie Well Furnished with Druggs"

In these increasingly bitter exchanges, each faction, as we have seen, sought justification for its own position by accusing the other side of either neglecting or cruelly exploiting patients of the humbler sort. No doubt a neutral observer, had one been on hand, would have found blame enough to distribute on both sides; for to the impoverished lower classes of seventeenth-century London, professional medical services of *any* sort were hard to come by. Still in force was the Elizabethan Poor Law of 1601, under which the poor might receive free medical help from the parish. But this help, even when available, was restricted to those born in the parish and still living there, which effectively excluded much of the metropolitan populace. There was also limited charity treatment available at such endowed hospitals as St. Batholomew's and St. Thomas's; but for a population the size of London's (about 700,000 at the close of the century) such facilities were far too few; nor did they make provision for cases not requiring hospitalization. For the most part, the sick poor of London simply went unattended, or else sought what help they could afford from the army of submedical quacks and unlicensed healers.[11]

In the numerous tracts generated by the hostility between physicians and apothecaries, descriptions of the plight of the poor were almost invariably accompanied by pious calls for more medical charity. In most instances, however, the charity thus advocated was conceived of as purely voluntary and dependent upon individual, rather than collective generosity.[12] It was not until 1670 that the idea of a public clinic to be supported and administered by the College of Physicians began to emerge. The earliest version of the plan seems to be that offered in *Some Papers Writ in the Year 1664. In Answer to a Letter, Concerning the Practice of Physick in England* (1670). The author, identified only as *"Dr. T.C.,"* urges his colleagues to establish a free dispensary, though he foresees that "The Charity there designed to supply all the poor . . . would be looked upon but as a design to Monopolise to the *Colledge,* and to invest the Physitians with a power to enslave *Chyrurgeons and Apothecaries."*[13] In the same year another scheme for a dispensary run by doctors (though this time with token fees and enlisting the help of apothecaries) was put forward in *The Accomplisht Physician,* whose anonymous author calls upon the college to appoint "one or two Junior Physicians in every Ward, whose visiting Fee they should be obliged by Oath, shall not exceed a shilling." In addition, the author proposes a *"Pharmacopoea Pauperum"* in which "two or three Apothecaries, authorized for that purpose," will prepare low cost prescriptions.[14]

In the quarter century that was to elapse before a charity clinic was actually established, several variations on these early schemes were proposed by physicians. From the first the Society of Apothecaries reacted to such plans with a skepticism that hardened into active opposition as the College of Physicians grew more purposeful in espousing the dispensary cause. In the course of the ensuing dispute, each side naturally sought to impugn the motives of the other. Thus, the dispensarians regularly pictured their opponents as men so greedy that they were unwilling to countenance even the slightest threat to their cruelly won profits. Conversely, the apothecaries characterized the dispensarians as arrogant physicians who, having long neglected the poor, now found that a spurious benevolence was a useful way of disguising the pursuit of professional advantage. To at least one contemporary observer, both factions were more or less correct in their unflattering views of each other's motives, and the whole dispensary dispute, in his opinion, boiled down to little more than a sordid business competition between two sets of traders: for "the Mystery and Bottom of the Business [is] no less than a War proclaimed by one Company of Merchants against another for interloping. . . ."[15]

A more detached view of the motives behind the dispensary movement suggests that its supporters were neither as exclusively altruistic as they claimed to be nor as meanly self-serving as their opponents would have it. There is no reason to question the sincerity of the humanitarian impulse which led so many physicians to become dispensarians. Indeed, many (like Garth) had long records of private benevolence to attest to their compassion. Moreover, beyond the general promptings of conscience, there was a more immediate ethical reason for doctors of the time to feel a sense of obligation to the poor. Whatever excuses and explanation might be offered, physicians could not easily deny that many of them had left London during the plague, and with this in mind, at least some in the college may well have viewed the dispensary as a kind of overdue expiatory gesture. However, motives are seldom pure in any complicated enterprise, and it is obvious that the dispensary scheme, aside from its moral virtues, strongly commended itself to physicians as a promising weapon against their professional rivals. *"Dr. T.C.,"* author of the original dispensary proposal, boasted that if his plan were adopted, "the next age will scarce know, what *an Apothecarie* is."[16] The hope of seeing that prophecy fulfilled no doubt helped to recruit a good many dispensarians for whom a simple call to Christian charity was insufficiently compelling.

The men who comprised the Society of Apothecaries, we may assume, were no less compassionate than those in the College of Physicians. But the history of feuding between the two groups had rendered the society, as one of its historians puts it, "hedgehog-like, all prickles on the slightest notice."[17] The society perceived all too clearly that one of the hoped for effects of a dispensary would be a drastic reduction in numbers and income for apothecaries. To men who had become used to thinking of *themselves* as the special friends of the sick poor, the suspiciously sudden benevolence being shown by physicians seemed little more than a cynical tactic in the college's long campaign to strip apothecaries of their livelihood and professional dignity.

It was five years after *"Dr. T.C."* and the author of *The Accomplisht Physician* had offered their proposals that the College of Physicians made its first official move toward establishment of a dispensary. On August 24, 1675, the college sent the Society of Apothecaries a document proclaiming a "cheerful readyness to advise and prescribe" to the poor at no charge. In furtherance of this good work, two members had been appointed to serve at specified times in the College Hall in Warwick Lane, and now the apothecaries were being called upon to "comply with our just and real intention and designe of serving the public in affording medicines prescribed by us to such poor at rates answerable to the lowness of their condition."[18] Accompanying this statement was a second document asking that the society send representatives to meet with the college in order to make the necessary arrangements. The first reaction of the society was to question the validity of the two documents, since neither had been formally signed by the college president or censors. Assured that the proposal was official, the suspicious apothecaries reluctantly agreed to meet the physicians as suggested. At that meeting, however, the society took deep offense when its emissaries were met by a single physician, rather than full committee. After so unpromising a start, negotiations soon bogged down in mutual recriminations, of which the proposed dispensary was an early casualty.

After a lapse of twelve years, however, the College of Physicians resumed the attack by formally announcing on July 28, 1687, that its members would henceforth give free treatment and advice to any certified pauper. In practical terms, this plan was less workable than the 1675 proposal, since no set place or hours were given, nor was any provision made for free or cheap medicines. Moreover, the apothecaries—already inclined to distrust physician-inspired schemes of medical philanthropy— were put in an even less cooperative mood by several provocative new statutes which the college concurrently adopted. Along with the usual denunciation of pharmacists turned practitioners, the new bylaws included one the apothecaries found especially offensive:

Because it is found by Experience that the Apothecaries from the Prescripts of Physicians, attain some pretence or shadow of false Knowledge (everywhere boasting themselves to Sick Persons) which they abuse . . . to their own profit; We Determine and Ordain, that no Collegue . . . add Directions as they call them, to their Prescripts . . . but he shall leave them with the Sick, or at least take care that they be first signed and carried to his house; in the mean time let him command, that the Medicines prescribed in the Scrowls be only signed with some agreeable [i.e., appropriate] titles or apt notes for their distinction, to the intent that . . . nothing at all be smelt out by this sort of Medicasters, with what design, intention, or for what uses the Remedies are prescribed.[19]

As the battle lines in the dispute became clearer, there began to emerge within the ranks of the college a significant minority of physicians who strongly opposed the prevailing dispensarian sentiment. These men, the so-called "Apothecaries Physicians," doubtless had motives as mixed as those of most other participants. Some, like the famous anatomist, Dr. Edward Tyson ("Dull *Carus*" in *The Dispensary*), honestly felt "that such dispensaries would work too sudden and great a hardship upon the apothecaries."[20] Others presumably saw no good reason to endanger the reciprocally advantageous relationships they had established with their apothecary colleagues. The dispensarians, predictably, took a more cynical view of the motives of dissenting physicians. As one anonymous pamphleteer explained: "Any *Citizen* who will give himself the *trouble* of *thinking* will easily hence *discern* the reason of the *perpetual Dissensions* of the *College*. When one party would raise up its *reputation* by serving the *Publick* faithfully, the other strenuously oppose all *Projects* of that kind, to merit the favour of the *Apothecaries*."[21]

Whatever the reasons for their opposition, the "Apothecaries Physicians" were never able to do more than temporarily thwart the majority will, though in the process they came to inspire as much, if not more, acrimony than the apothecaries themselves.

The growing sense of division within the college ranks first shows itself in the *Annals* for August 23, 1687, when members were ordered not to "reveal or divulge the Secrets of the Colledge" to outsiders.[22] On the same occasion, the *Annals* reprove certain unnamed physicians who, "for the sake of snatching a mean and sordid practice,"[23] have allied themselves with the apothecaries. The factionalism in the college surfaced more openly at the meeting of December 22, 1687, when it was proposed that if an apothecary refused to submit his bills to the college for approval, those bills be declared incompetent. "But some heats arising between some of the Members of the College, fitter to be forgott than registred, nothing concerning this Order was done."[24]

On August 13, 1688, the dispensarians, finding their earlier resolution for free treatment to the poor was ineffective, reendorsed the idea of setting up a drug repository where indigent patients would receive medicines at minimal cost. The Society of Apothecaries, however, was still unwilling to submit to college control, and so refused to cooperate in this scheme. In hopes of settling grievances, the society approached the college in March, 1690, with a proposition of its own: if the college would abrogate certain of its offensive antiapothecary statutes and if its members would agree not to practice pharmacy, the society would undertake to keep apothecaries from treating patients.[25] But the college, aware that existing laws on the subject had proved unenforceable, was no more receptive to this overture than the apothecaries had been to earlier initiatives by the physicians.

In the face of their inability to put through a workable plan, the dispensarians could only withdraw and wait for a more propitious time to renew their efforts. That time came early in 1695, when antagonism between physician and apothecary once again flared up. The immediate provocation for resumed hostilities came in the course of parliamentary hearings on a petition in which the Society of Apothecaries asked that its members be exempted (as doctors had long been) from jury service and other parish duties. In arguing on behalf of this proposition, Sir William Williams (the society's counsel, who figures as "Vagellius" in *The Dispensary*) tactlessly maintained that in any assessment of comparative social utility, apothecaries would be found superior to physicians in benevolence, public spirit, and even medical skills. When word of these remarks reached the College of Physicians, one immediate response was a resolution reviving earlier plans for a charity clinic and drug repository. This time, as a sign of its desire for action, the college appointed a five-man "Committee on Medicines" to implement the proposals. The chairman of this distinguished group was Dr. Hans Sloane, and among its members was the man who would shortly become the best-known dispensarian of all—Dr. Samuel Garth.

In June of 1695 the college turned for support to the lord mayor, aldermen, and Common Council of London. At a meeting with council representatives on July 24, the physicians announced that they had compiled a list of some forty apothecaries who had pledged their willingness to fill charity prescriptions at a price set by the doctors. In response, the Society of Apothecaries denounced such arrangements and brought pressure to bear on the forty enemy sympathizers in its ranks, eventually forcing them to retract their promises of cooperation. Instead, the society put forth its own newest counterplan, offering to sell medicines to the poor at cost if the college would concede apothecaries the right, in the absence of a physician, to "give all the Assistance they are capable of by administring such remedies as may be necessary."[26] But the college, still adamantly opposed to allowing apothecaries to practice medicine under any circumstances, summarily rejected this plan.

Thus confronted with yet another impasse, the dispensarians decided to change their tactics. The new approach may have been suggested by an inquiry from the Common Council, which had asked whether, in view of the apothecaries' recalcitrance, the college itself might not be willing to provide, as well as prescribe the medicines at charity clinics. This plan, which had the advantage of circumventing the apothecaries completely, was warmly debated at the college meeting of August 12, 1695, and although "there were some fellows [who] threw up their Balls, and refused to ballot,"[27] fifty-eight members (including Garth) voted their approval in principle. Dissension in the college was strong enough to delay further progress for a year, but in late 1696 the dispensarians won an important victory. In November the Committee on Medicines submitted a resolution calling upon members to contribute not only their approval, but some ten pounds each toward "the furnishing [of] a Repository of Medicines, out of wch the poor shall be supplied. . . ."[28] On December 26, 1696, this subscription was endorsed by thirty-two members—a number that had grown to fifty-three by late 1698. Among the first signers, naturally, was Samuel Garth, who proudly reprinted the entire document in the second and all subsequent editions of *The Dispensary.*

Having raised the money to pay for drugs—and thus eliminated the need for cooperation from apothecaries—the dispensarians had in effect finally won their long-fought war. All that remained to make the charity clinic a reality was the working out of practical details, such as the arrangement in early 1697 whereby dispensary subscribers were leased a laboratory and two other rooms in the College Hall. The opposition continued to fight a delaying action, but by September 17, 1697, when Garth delivered his *Oratio Laudatoria,* his remarks made it clear that the question of a "Repositorie well furnished with Druggs for the help of the Poor" was no longer in doubt. To the dissident "Apothecaries Physicians" Garth pointedly says: ". . . in this I beseech you be comfortable; unlesse things . . . be come to this passe, that our keenest enemies are to be found at home. . . ."[29]

In the spring of 1698, the dispensary, suitably furnished and staffed, was at last ready to receive its first patients. To publicize the opening, the London *Post-Boy* (April 14-16) announced that: "The members of the College of Physicians have collected (by way of a Charitable Subscription) a Joynt-stock of about 500 l. to prepare at the said College all sorts of Medicines for the Poor, and to give them at the intrinsick Vallue, that is, for what they only cost, which will save the Poor 15 s. in the Pound; the Physicians have likewise obligated themselves voluntarily, under a forfeiture, to attend the College in turns, to give Advice to all People that will come thither for nothing, every Wednesday and Saturday in the Afternoon, all the year." Demand proved so brisk that soon two more dispensaries were opened, one in St. Martin's Lane, Westminister, and the other in Grace-Church Street, Cornhill. Contemporary estimates of the numbers of patients treated vary, but even the more conservative figures show an impressive 85,191 prescriptions filled in the first six and a half years of operation.[30]

The antidispensarians suffered a second blow with the publication in May, 1699, of Garth's *The Dispensary*. So well-received was the poem that two historians of the Society of Apothecaries credit Garth with having all but chased the opposition from the field. Barrett remarks that the whole dispute, "prolonged and undignified as it had been, . . . was killed by the efforts of Dr., afterwards Sir Samuel, Garth."[31] To this we may add Underwood's comment that, after publication of Garth's poem, "the active opposition to the Dispensary virtually subsided."[32] But such statements, however flattering to Garth, are misleading insofar as they imply that the opponents of a charity clinic were silenced by his work: for all its undeniable success, Garth's poem was repeatedly "answered" and denounced; nor did the newly established dispensaries themselves go long uncriticized by the "Apothecaries Physicians" and their allies.

During the early years of their operation, the dispensaries were sharply attacked in such works as *The Present Ill State of the Practice of Physick In This Nation* (1702), *Tentamen Medicinale* (1704), and *The Censor Censur'd: or The Antidote Examin'd* (1704). In these and similar tracts, the familiar charges of the old dispute were reiterated, and the new dispensaries dismissed as pious swindles. Thus, Ned Ward explains how physicians

Practice themselves, what they Blame and Condemn in others. And that the Town may not be deceiv'd by *Apothecaries*, they have made themselves *Medicine-Mongers*, under a pretence of serving the Publick with more Faithful Preparations; in order to perswade the World to a Belief of which, they have Publish'd Bills, where, in the true *Quacks Dialect*, they tell you the Poor shall be supply'd for nothing; but who ever is so Needy as to make a Challenge of their Promise empty Handed, will find, according to the *Mountebanks* Saying, *No Money, No Cure*.[33]

The dispensarian defense and counterattack came in such works as *The State of Physick in London* (1698), *The Necessity and Usefulness of the Dispensaries* (1702), and Robert Pitt's *The Antidote: Or, The Preservative of Health and Life* (1704). The pamphlet war continued heatedly until about 1705, when the dispute began to subside—partly because the dispensaries had by then amply shown their usefulness, and partly because in the previous year the apothecaries had been considerably mollified by an important legal victory. The College of Physicians had brought charges against one William Rose, an apothecary, for the illegal practice of medicine. Originally found guilty, Rose appealed to the House of Lords, and on March 15, 1704, his conviction was reversed, thus formally establishing the right of apothecaries to treat patients.

Having ceased after 1705 to be objects of active controversy, the dispensaries settled down to a twenty-year period of quietly serving the indigent. Little is known of these latter years of the dispensaries or of the reasons which finally led to their discontinuance. By June of 1725, however, only the Warwick Lane dispensary was still in operation, and when its lease came up for renewal, the College of Physicians appointed a committee to consider the matter. The committee deliberations were not recorded, but a combination of factors seems to have weighed against continuance. With the passage of time and the death of many of the original sponsors, the charitable impulse behind the movement had weakened. Moreover, new hospitals which performed equivalent charities were being founded in the city. Likewise, the usefulness of the dispensary as a means of keeping apothecaries in their place had been much diminished by the Rose case decision. In the light of these considerations, the committee recommended that the lease be withdrawn. The college members concurred, and on April 20, 1726, the "London Dispensary for the Sick-Poor" unobtrusively expired.

III *"The Muse that sung the Frogs in Arms"*

In the preface which he added to the second edition of *The Dispensary,* Garth explains that the idea for the comic "battle" in his poem was suggested by an actual scuffle or "feud that happened in the Dispensary, betwixt a member of the college with his retinue, and some of the servants that attended there to dispense the medicines."[34] Struck by the satiric possibilities of this unseemly incident (which presumably involved an irate "Apothecaries Physician"), Garth was inspired to expand the original, trivial altercation into the comic battle around which he composed the first full-scale mock-epic poem in the English language.

In brief, the major events in *The Dispensary* are as follows: canto 1, after a formal invocation and proposition, opens with a description of the history and original lofty purpose of the College of Physicians. In recent years, however, the college has been rendered ineffectual by factionalism, and accordingly, the god Sloth has taken up drowsy residence in its headquarters in Warwick Lane. But Sloth's slumbers are roughly interrupted by the sounds of the new dispensary being built, which prompts him to deliver a long speech of complaint. Sloth ends his speech (and the canto) by sending his servant, Phantom, to ask for help from the goddess Envy. In canto 2 Phantom finds Envy, whose baleful appearance and grotto are pictured in detail. Upon receipt of Sloth's message, Envy assumes the shape of Colon, an apothecary, and goes to visit Horoscope, another apothecary, in his shop. After a description of Horoscope's shop and the pathetic customers awaiting his services, Envy arrives and informs the apothecary of the newly built dispensary. Overcome by the prospect of a loss of income, Horoscope faints and is finally revived only when his assistant, Squirt, applies the vapors from a urinal.

As canto 3 opens, Horoscope broods through a sleepless night wondering what action to take. By morning, he is resolved to fight, and he sends Squirt to call all the apothecaries together for a meeting. In the meantime, Horoscope builds an altar to Disease, whose help he solicits for the coming struggle. Ominously, the goddess ignores his prayers, and the altar collapses. The scene then shifts to the meeting in Apothecaries' Hall, where the assemblage is addressed in turn by Diasenna (who urges conciliation), Colocynthis (who advocates a fight to the death), and Ascarides (who suggests a middle course — subversion of the dispensary in collusion with disaffected physicians). The proceedings end in confusion when a supply of fulminate of gold stored in the basement explodes.

In the beginning of canto 4 we move to Covent Garden, where Mirmillo, a physician who espouses the apothecaries' cause, has gathered with other antidispensarian doctors to discuss strategy. Horoscope, chastened by his earlier failure to invoke Disease, urges caution. The Bard (Sir Richard Blackmore) sneers at Horoscope's ineffectiveness, and recites a few lines of his own poetry, which at once brings forth the goddess. Disease, after some critical remarks about the Bard's verse, indicates her

The Historical and Literary Background

willingness to help in the fight. In a long passage added to the sixth edition (1706), Disease then raises a whirlwind which transports Horoscope to the Fortunate Islands, there to consult the goddess Fortune. The trip is described in detail, and the canto ends with Fortune cryptically prophecying success and failure for both sides in the fight.

As canto 5 begins, we find Mirmillo (like Horoscope in canto 3) spending a sleepless night worrying about the coming confrontation. The goddess Discord, however, assumes the shape of Querpo, one the the antidispensarian physicians, and issues an eloquent call to arms that soon restores Mirmillo's militancy. At dawn Mirmillo joins the army of apothecaries and sympathetic physicians, who are described in detail as they gather for a surprise attack. However, the goddess Fame warns the physicians of the enemy approach, and after a quick council at Warwick Lane, the dispensarians turn to meet the foe. The furious battle—in which the weapons are syringes, gally-pots, phials, and other medical paraphernalia—is described at length. Eventually, as the apothecaries begin to get the upper hand, Querpo is poised to slay Stentor, the leader of the physicians. However, Apollo stops the fatal blow by assuming the form of a "Fee," at which Querpo instinctively grabs, thus dropping his weapon.

At the beginning of canto 6, the goddess Health appears, stops the fighting, and instructs Celsus, a physician, to accompany her to the Elysian Fields in order to ask the shade of Harvey how the issue should be settled. The bulk of this final canto is devoted to a description of the journey to the underworld and an account of the various spirits encountered en route. At last the travelers reach Harvey, who advises the college to place its trust in Atticus (Lord Somers, president of the Royal Society and lord chancellor of England), who will restore the healing arts to their former dignity. The poem ends as Celsus and Health withdraw to convey Harvey's message to the college.[35]

The mock-heroic mode, as employed in *The Dispensary*, derives its central effect by violating the principle of literary decorum that requires a congruence between subject matter and style. When a conspicuously prosaic, trivial, or sordid topic is dealt with in lofty and dignified terms, the resultant discrepancy between matter and manner creates a built-in comic contrast. In its most rudimentary and diffuse form, as a passing sarcasm or casual verbal irony, the mock-heroic is surely one of the commonest techniques of ridicule in English literature. More sustained efforts, however, in which the comic contrast between form and content functions as the dominant strategy for an entire work, are comparatively few in English prior to the late seventeenth century. Some of the more noteworthy older examples of extended mock-heroics are Chaucer's *Nun's Priest's Tale* (1380) and *Sir Thopas* (1387), William Dunbar's *Turnament* (1507), Michael Drayton's *Nymphidia* (1627), Edmund Waller's *Battle of the Summer Isles* (1645), and Dryden's *MacFlecknoe* (1681). Samuel Butler's *Hudibras* (1663, 1664, 1678) is sometimes loosely classified as mock-heroic, but may more properly be described as a kind of travesty, which (in a reversal of the mock-heroic approach) uses a deliberate lowness of language and imagery to ridicule its subject's pretensions to dignity.[36]

However, except for Dryden's influence (discussed below), the native mock-heroic tradition contributed relatively little to Garth's poem, most of whose major antecedents and analogues come from across the English channel. For *The Dispensary* is not merely a mock-heroic poem; it is more specifically a mock-*epic* poem, and the humorous epic, like its serious counterpart, originated and developed on the Continent. As a genre, the mock-epic may claim a pedigree scarcely less venerable than that of the ancient prototypes whose specialized diction, conventions, and techniques it satirizes. Indeed, according to Aristotle in *De Poetica,* Homer himself composed the first comic epic: the lost *Margites.* Also traditionally attributed to Homer (though recent scholarship suggests a later origin) is *Batrachomyomachia,* in which a battle between frogs and mice is presented in high heroic style, complete with invocation, extended similes, divine intervention, and other devices associated with the formal epic. Although the influence of *Batrachomyomachia* on *The Dispensary* is only of the most general sort, Garth does acknowledge the example of the older poem when (in a line added to canto 5 in the sixth edition) he remarks that an adequate description of the gathered armies would require the eloquence of "the Muse that sung the frogs in Arms."[37]

A more nearly contemporary European example of the mock-epic was Alessandro Tassoni's twelve canto *La Secchia Rapita*

(1622), which deals satirically with a thirteenth-century war between Modena and Bologna. Building on the tradition that the war had been instigated by the theft of a bucket, Tassoni parodies the dispute by assuming the epic manner (and in places the actual language) of Homer, Vergil, Ariosto, and Tasso. Although *La Secchia Rapita* won praise from Dryden and Rowe as a milestone in the evolution of the mock-epic, it was evidently far from popular in England, where it was not translated until 1710, and then only partially. On the whole, it would seem that Tassoni's poem, like the *Batrachomyomachia,* had little direct influence upon Garth beyond helping to define the developing mock-epic as a genre.

IV *"To Polish English Sense With Foreign Wit"*

Of Garth's predecessors, the one who contributed by far the most to *The Dispensary* was Nicolas Boileau-Despréaux, whose *Le Lutrin* originally appeared in four cantos in 1674, and achieved its final form with the addition of two further cantos in 1683. In *Le Lutrin* Garth found an invaluable model of mock-epic structure and technique.[38] Boileau's poem, like Garth's, was inspired by an actual incident—a dispute in the church of Sainte Chapelle over the placing of a lectern—and even a brief summary of the French work indicates its numerous points of similarity to *The Dispensary.*

Le Lutrin begins with a formal invocation of the Muse, after which the poet describes how the goddess Discorde, distressed to see Sainte Chapelle so peaceful when all other French churches are divided by bitter feuding, approaches the church's ambitious Tresorier in a dream and incites him to rivalry with the Chantre. Once stirred up, the Tresorier resolves to place a large desk in the choir loft so as to obscure the Chantre during services. The church personnel divide into opposing camps over the question of the placement of the desk, and various Furies and personified abstractions join in the dispute. Great assemblies are held, and each leader addresses his followers at length. All this unaccustomed activity disturbs the somnolent goddess Mollesse, who delivers a long speech of complaint. Meanwhile Nuit, angered that the agents of the Tresorier plan to install the desk under cover of her darkness, secretly hides an owl in the desk drawer. When the owl suddenly flies out, the Tresorier's men at first flee in confusion, but after Discorde revives their courage, they return and place the desk in the chantry. The next morning the Chantre and his allies, after holding a formal debate about tactics, respond by chopping the desk to splinters. Eventually the two factions meet in epic battle, using books as their weapons. The Chantre's forces prove superior, but the tide of battle is dramatically reversed when the Tresorier raises his hand as if in blessing. Instinctively his opponents fall to their knees, and in this position they are easily defeated. Meanwhile, Piété, who has long since fled Sainte Chapelle, appeals to Themis, the goddess of Justice. Themis recommends Ariste (M. de Lamoignon—a friend and patron of Boileau), and the poem concludes as he settles the dispute by arbitration.

The close resemblances between *The Dispensary* and *Le Lutrin* naturally did not escape Garth's contemporaries. In a letter dated May 21, 1699—only two weeks after the first publication of *The Dispensary*—W[illiam] A[dams] writes to Thomas Tanner: "As to the Satyr you mention of Dr. Garth's, I've seen it: but understand it not perfectly. You must in your next letter give me a kind of Key &c. There are good whims in it, and the man seems to have a genius for poetry, but not overmuch judgmt. in the managemt. of it. It is an imitation of Boileau's Lutrin, but vastly short on't."[39] It was presumably in response to similar comments that Garth included in the preface to the second edition an answer to the critics who accused him of having "imitated the Lutrin of Monsieur Boileau. I must own, I am proud of the imputation; unless their quarrel be, that I have not done it enough: but he that will give himself the trouble of examining, will find I have copied him in nothing but in two or three lines in the complaint of Molesse, Canto II, and in one in his first Canto; the sense of which line is entirely his, and I could wish it were not the only good one in mine."[40]

Garth's contention that his debt to Boileau was insignificant seems to have convinced no one. Indeed, in the eyes of Garth's enemies, Boileau's contribution loomed so large as to make *The Dispensary* little better than plagiarism. Blackmore, in *A Satyr Against Wit* (1699), contemptuously refers to "felonious *Garth*," who "Smuggles French Wit, as others Silks and Wine."[41] Similarly, Defoe, in *The Pacificator* (1700), refers to "Whole Wings of Foreign Troops" that:

> ... *Garth* from *France* to Wits assistance drew,
> Something the Matter was those Troops betraid 'em;
> He ill Procur'd them, or he had not Paid 'em;
> 'Twas a dull fancy in him to think fit,
> To polish English Sense with Foreign Wit.[42]

Less prejudiced critics took a more moderate position, but even Garth's admirers stressed how much he owed to Boileau. Thus, Nicholas Rowe, in the *Account of Boileau's Writings* he wrote as a preface to John Ozell's 1708 translation of *Le Lutrin*, remarks: "And since I have mentioned [*Le Lutrin* and *The Dispensary*] together, it may not be improper to observe that, in the latter of them, though writ upon a very different subject, there are some passages that are plainly imitations or indeed even translations of the former: those who will take the trouble to compare them, now they are both in one language, will be best able to judge how near the translator of *Le Lutrin* comes to the beauties which all the world has so justly admired in Dr. Garth. . . ."[43] Likewise, Joseph Spence, in his *Quelques Remarques Hist: sur les Poëtes Anglois* (ca. 1732), says that "*Garth, dans sa Dispensarie, a bien imité le Lutrin de Boileau,*" [44] and Joseph Warton, in *An Essay on the Genius of Pope* (1756) characterizes *The Dispensary* as "a palpable imitation of the *Lutrin.*"[45]

Of those who noted *The Dispensary*'s debt to Boileau, not all shared Adams's view that the former fell "vastly short" of the latter. In his *Letters of Wit, Politicks, and Morality* (1701), Abel Boyer says of Garth: "He has writ a Poem in *English*, call'd the *Dispensary;* wherein he has equall'd, if not exceeded the *Lutrin*, which he had proposed to himself as a Model. . . ."[46] Boyer's opinion was no doubt influenced by his personal friendship to Garth, but no such bias can be attributed to Voltaire, who, in his *Dictionnaire Philosophique* (1764), is even more emphatic: "La poème de Garth sur les médecins et les apothicaires est moins dans le style burlesque que dans celui du *Lutrin* de Boileau: on y trouve beaucoup plus d'imagination, de variété, de naiveté, etc., que dans le *Lutrin;* et ce qui est étonnant, c'est qu'une profonde érudition y est embellie par la finesse et par les graces. . . ."[47]

In our own day, critics have been less generous than Voltaire, and at least one has come close to endorsing Blackmore's view of "felonious *Garth*" decked out in borrowed poetic finery: "Das *Dispensary*," writes Theodor Schenk, "ist eine direkte, ziemlich genaue nachahmung des Boileauschen *Lutrin*[;] es ist überhaupt von allen nachahmungen desselben die ähnlichste. . . ."[48] In support of this contention, Schenk offers some seventeen pages of parallel quotations selected to illustrate how Garth echoes Boileau's language and sense. In the great majority of cases, however, Schenk's examples are anything but convincing, based, as they most frequently are, on vaguely analogous word patterns, diffusely similar sentiments, or tenuously equated metaphors. Moreover, even in those instances where a demonstrable parallel can be shown, it does not always follow (as Schenk assumes) that Garth is directly imitating Boileau: for between any two authors parodying the same handful of epic models, one might reasonably expect to find a certain number of purely fortuitous analogues.

To reject Schenk's exaggerated view of Garth's dependence on Boileau, however, is not to accept Garth's own disingenuous claim that he drew on *Le Lutrin* for nothing more than three or four lines. A more accurate assessment comes from A. F. B. Clark, who has carefully compared the two poems and concluded that although "*The Dispensary* is very far indeed from being a mere imitation of the *Lutrin* . . . , it is perfectly clear that [Garth] had the general scheme and method of the *Lutrin* before his eyes all the time."[49] In his examination of the two works, Clark cites general similarities of structure and approach, particular parallels of character, plot, and technique, and finally, the relatively few passages in which Garth's language and thought clearly have been adapted from Boileau.

As the reactions of Garth's contemporaries show, certain general points of resemblance between *Le Lutrin* and *The Dispensary* are at once apparent. Thus, both poems are divided into six cantos; both deal satirically with professional groups whose sordid bickering belies their pretence to selfless dedication; each poem employs in similar fashion such traditional epic features as invocation of the muse, extended simile, supernatural machinery, solemn councils, formal speeches, and a climactic battle of contending heroes. It should also be noted that in the final canto of each poem, the satire gives way to straightforward description and exhortation. Yet, such broad points of congruence, though suggestive, do not by themselves prove very much, since many of them are the kind of generic resemblances inevitable in any two mock-epics. It is in the more specific analogies that the nature of Garth's use of *Le Lutrin* emerges.

Of the more particular similitudes between *The Dispensary* and *Le Lutrin*, one of the most noticeable lies in the major characters. Like Boileau, Garth makes heavy use of personified abstractions, and in some cases these bear an unmistakable family resemblance to their French originals. There is an obvious connection, for example, between Boileau's Mollesse and Garth's Sloth—both deliver similar peevish complaints at their disturbed repose; both serve as incongruous vehicles for royal panegyrics (addressed to Louis XIV and William III respectively); and both are finally obliged in their indolence to seek help from others. Likewise, Garth's Envy corresponds in many ways to both Boileau's Chicane and Discorde—more especially the latter, whom Envy also emulates by taking on human form so as better to foment trouble. Garth's human characters, based as they mostly are on actual persons, show less resemblance to Boileau's than do the allegorical figures. However, Horoscope and Mirmillo in *The Dispensary* may be said to be like the Tresorier and Chantre of *Le Lutrin* in that all four are dominated by similar kinds of greed and vanity, and each is served by a devoted assistant. Just as Boileau's Chantre passes a sleepless night worrying about the coming battle, so in Garth, both Horoscope and Mirmillo spend analogous nights, and each, when he finally arises, sends off his servant (as did the Chantre) to call for an assembly of followers. Moreover, in both poems the final resolution to the action comes (after equivalent comic battles) in like fashion: Boileau's Themis advises Piété to seek out Ariste; even as Garth's Harvey tells Health to consult Atticus—each poet using the occasion to depict a personal friend in the flattering role of peacemaker.

In addition to the parallels already indicated, *The Dispensary* contains a number of distinct verbal echoes of *Le Lutrin*. The majority of these are brief, and in them Garth's appropriations are limited to an occasional felicitous simile, descriptive phrase, or rhetorical flourish.[50] In at least one instance, however, borrowing of a more extensive sort occurs. As mentioned earlier, Garth's Sloth is modeled on Boileau's Mollesse, and there are obvious similarities in such passages as the descriptions of their respective abodes (*The Dispensary*, I, 71-84; *Le Lutrin*, I, 57-68 and II, 97-108) and in the accounts of how each arises from interrupted slumbers (*The Dispensary*, I, 101-4; *Le Lutrin*, II,

117-20).[51] Like Mollesse, Sloth delivers a lament, and Garth himself (as quoted earlier) concedes (albeit inadequately) that he "copied" Boileau in "some two or three lines." In point of fact, both the sense and a good deal of the language in Sloth's speech follow the French original—as, for example, in such passages as those wherein each complains of how the current monarch (unlike his predecessors) has proved distressingly immune to her blandishments:

> Ce doux siecle n'est plus. Le Ciel impitoyable
> A placé sur leur Trône un Prince infatigable.
> Il brave mes douceurs, il est sourd à ma voix:
> Tous les jours il m'éveille au bruit de ses exploits.
> Rien ne peut arrester sa vigilante audace.
> L'Esté n'a point de feux, l'Hyver n'a point de glace.
> (II, 133-38)

> But that, the Great *Nassau's* Heroick Arms
> Has long prevented with his loud Alarms.
> Still my Indulgence with contempt he flies,
> His Couch a Trench, his Canopy the Skies.
> Nor Skies nor Seasons his Resolves controul,
> Th'*Aequator* has no Heat, no Ice the *Pole*.
> (I, 137-42)

In sum, the evidence shows that *The Dispensary* owes much of its general scheme, some of its characters, and a few of its particular passages to *Le Lutrin*. It would be misleading, however, to stress the similarities between the two works without calling some attention to their considerable differences of plot, style, structure, and tone. Of such differences, perhaps the most significant are those reflecting Garth's systematic enhancement of the "epic" aspects of his poem. Thus, as opposed to Boileau's intermittently high style, Garth adds an important dimension to *The Dispensary* by carefully sustaining the heroic diction and language throughout. Garth's formal speeches and harangues, for example, are not only more elaborate and imposing than those of Boileau, they are much more faithfully Homeric or Vergilian in manner. In like fashion, whereas Boileau's narrative style is for the most part dry, straightforward, and unadorned, Garth reenforces his epic tone by including much detailed description, either of the picturesque (as in the account of Horoscope's shop in canto 2) or of the sublime (as in the journey to the Fortunate Isles in canto 4).

Structurally as well as stylistically *The Dispensary* is a more carefully thought out and integrated mock-epic than *Le Lutrin*. In Boileau's work, the battle is merely incidental, and it takes place only by pure chance when the rival forces happen to meet unexpectedly in front of a book store. In *The Dispensary*, on the other hand, the battle (like its epic prototypes) is a much-anticipated, studiously planned for event at the center of the action, and accordingly Garth is able to include (as Boileau cannot) appropriately satiric versions of such epic conventions as the heroic boast, the debate of battlefield strategy, and the arming of individual heroes. Nor is there anything in *Le Lutrin* analogous to Garth's inclusion in canto 6 of that traditional epic feature, the descent into the netherworld. It may be said, then, that although Boileau's poem served Garth as an invaluable source of ideas and a model for emulation, of the two works, *The Dispensary* is the more fully conceived and rendered mock-epic, and as such represents a distinct advancement of the genre over *Le Lutrin*.

V *"Laughing a Folly out of Countenance"*

Next to Boileau, the most significant literary influence upon Garth was that of his old friend and poetic mentor, John Dryden. In the late seventeenth century, Dryden's example and precepts had served to introduce in England a new satiric mode, elements of which Garth found eminently adaptable to his own purposes. Of Dryden's poetical works, the most immediately useful to Garth were *Absalom and Achitophel* (1681) and *MacFlecknoe* (1682), both of which offered important object lessons in comic tone, authorial stance, and the effective use of heroic style in satire. Beyond such general matters, Dryden's influence on *The Dispensary* is most readily apparent in the areas of verse technique, ironic characterization, and descriptive approach.[52]

In his *Discourse Concerning the Original and Progress of Satire* (1693), Dryden had strongly recommended "the verse of ten syllables, which we call the English heroic" as the meter best suited to "manly satire."[53] By way of illustration, Dryden's own poetic practice had already shown how well the closed iambic pentameter couplet could function as a vehicle for epigram, antithesis, symmetry, and other satirically desirable effects. In *The Dispensary,* Garth follows Dryden's advice and example, both as to meter and in overall verse technique. Thus we find a perceptibly Drydenesque cadence and structure in the poem's prosody. Garth's adaptation of Dryden's versification, however, is more than merely imitative; for in Garth's hands the heroic couplet takes on a new regularity and definition. In its metrics, *The Dispensary,* as George Saintsbury points out,

represents, as a sort of practical *Ars Poetica* . . . , the stage between Dryden and Pope, and, without exaggeration, may be said to be the first draft—and not a very rough first draft—of the couplet versification and the poetic diction which were to dominate the whole eighteenth century. There was nothing in Garth even distantly approaching the genius of Dryden or the genius of Pope; but he had learnt from Dryden all that Dryden could teach to a younger contemporary of more than ordinary talent, and he anticipated Pope in most things that did not require Pope's special gifts. The smooth running couplets with a clinching stamp at the close; the well-marked pause in the centre of each line; the balanced epithets in the respective halves, . . .—all these things appear. And, in some passages, such as Horoscope's flight to Teneriffe and the descent of Hygeia to the shades, the method is shown almost within reach of its best. . . .[54]

Dryden's example also helped to influence Garth's techniques of characterization, most especially in his use of the satiric personality sketch. Thus, in Garth's formal descriptions of the major antidispensarians, we find rhythms and accents similar to those used by Dryden in his urbanely acid portraits of the conspirators in *Absalom and Achitophel.* Perhaps one example will suffice to illustrate the nature of this parallel. Dryden describes Achitophel as

> For close Designs, and crooked Counsels fit;
> Sagacious, Bold, and Turbulent of wit:
> Restless, unfixt in Principles and Place;
> In Power unpleas'd, impatient of Disgrace.
> A firey Soul, which working out its way,
> Fretted the Pigmy Body to decay:
> And o'r inform'd the Tenement of Clay.
> A daring Pilot in extremity;
> Pleas'd with the Danger, when the Waves went high

> He sought the Storms; but for a Calm unfit,
> Would Steer too nigh the Sands, to boast his Wit.
>   (152-162)[55]

To this we may compare the tone and pattern of Garth's description of Urim (added to canto 1 in the fifth edition):

> Urim was civil, and not void of sense,
> Had humour, and a courteous Confidence.
> So spruce he moves, so gracefully he cocks;
> The hallow'd Rose declares him Orthodox.
> He pass'd his easie Hours, instead of Pray'r,
> In Madrigals, and Phillising the Fair.
> Constant at Feasts, and each Decorum knew,
> As soon as the Dessert appear'd, withdrew.
> Always obliging and without offence,
> And fancy'd for his gay Impertinence.
>   (T.N., 729)[56]

In addition to the resemblances already cited, Garth reflects Dryden's technique (and approximates his language as well) in the descriptions applied to certain symbolic locales. In *MacFlecknoe*, for example, Dryden introduces Barbican as follows:

> Close to the Walls which fair *Augusta* bind,
> (The fair *Augusta* much to fears inclin'd)
> An ancient fabrick, rais'd t'inform the sight,
> There stood of yore, and *Barbican* it hight:
> A watch Tower once; but now, so Fate ordains,
> Of all the Pile an empty name remains.
>   (64-69)

Garth reflects these lines in his description of the College of Physicians building in Warwick Lane:

> Not far from that most celebrated Place,
> Where angry Justice shews her awful Face;
> Where little Villains must submit to Fate,
> That great Ones may enjoy the World in state;
> There stands a Dome, Majestick to the Sight,
> And sumptuous Arches bear its oval Height;

> A golden Globe plac'd high with artful Skill,
> Seems, to the distant Sight, a gilded Pill.
>
> (I, 7-14)

In analogous fashion, Dryden's description of the theater in *MacFlecknoe*

> Near these a Nursery erects its head,
> Where Queens are form'd, and future Hero's bred;
> Where unfledg'd Actors learn to laugh and cry,
> Where infant Punks their tender Voices try,
> And little *Maximins* the Gods defy.
> Great *Fletcher* never treads in Buskins here,
> Nor greater *Johnson* dares in Socks appear—
>
> (74-80)

seems to have provided Garth the model for his description of Covent Garden:

> Not far from that most famous Theater,
> Where wandring Punks each Night at five repair;
> Where Purple Emperors in Buskins tread,
> And Rule imaginary Worlds for Bread;
> Where *Bently*, by Old Writers, wealthy grew,
> And *Briscoe* lately was undone by New.
>
> (IV, 1-6)

To such parallels of technique and language may be added a less specific, but no less important aspect of Dryden's influence upon *The Dispensary*; for Garth profited not only from Dryden's practice, but also from his critical writings concerning satire. Prior to Dryden's time, satire in England had been traditionally perceived as a literary mode whose essence lay in deliberate lowness of language and tone. In part, this attitude derived from earlier critics who, having traced the word "satire" to the Greek "satyr," went on to argue that a harsh and abusive manner (appropriate to an uncouth woodland deity) was an intrinsic element in the satirist's art. Dryden, however, rejected this etymology, and suggested that "satire" came from the descriptive Latin phrase "lanx satura" or "varigated dish." Instead of viewing satire as an inherently "low" form, Dryden hailed it as a species of heroic poetry, and as such, capable of equivalent virtues and subject to similar rules. Thus, Dryden argued that "a perfect satire," no less than a serious heroic poem, should have a beginning, middle, and end; should focus upon a single subject to be treated in a single major plot line; should be composed in heroic couplets; and should display in its diction the "beautiful turns of words and thoughts, which are as requisite in this, as in heroic poetry itself . . ."(II, 108).[57] Above all, Dryden called upon the satirist to do his job with grace, elegance, and wit: "How easy is it to call rogue and villain, and that wittily! But how hard to make a man appear a fool, a blockhead, or a knave, without using any of those opprobrious terms! . . . there is still a vast difference betwixt the slovenly butchering of a man, and the fineness of a stroke that separates the head from the body, and leaves it standing in its place"(II, 92-3).

Finally, having commended satire to his contemporaries as a dignified genre, Dryden offered a strong inducement to would-be satirists by suggesting that satire was one of the few literary forms in which modern writers might hope to excel over those of classical antiquity. In support of this claim, he cited Boileau and the earl of Dorset (to whom the *Discourse* was dedicated) as satirists superior to those of Greece and Rome. Though few subsequent critics have been willing to rate Dorset so highly, there were many in the eighteenth century who echoed Dryden's opinion as to the preeminence of modern satire—more specifically modern English satire as developed by Garth and Pope. Thus, Joseph Warton, writing in *The Adventurer*, No. 133 (February 12, 1754), remarked: "Above all, the *Lutrin*, the *Rape of the Lock*, the *Dispensatory* [sic] and the *Dunciad*, cannot be paralleled by any works that the wittiest of the ancients can boast of: for by assuming the form of the epopea, they have acquired a dignity and gracefulness, which all satires delivered merely in the poet's own person must want, and with which the satirists of antiquity were wholly unacquainted."[58] Similarly, Thomas Powell, in *Emma, or the Baculiniad* (ca. 1805), reported that "My Lord *Orford* [Horace Walpole] declared that the *Rape of the Lock*, the *Dispensary*, and the *Lutrin*, were three poems unrivalled for elegance by any antient or modern productions. Every competent reader must set his seal to that testimony."[59]

In canto 4 of *The Dispensary*, the goddess Fury lectures Sir Richard Blackmore on poetic excellence, and she advises him (among other things) to "consider *Dryden* well" (IV, 211) before presuming to set pen to paper. That Garth himself had followed Fury's counsel is apparent throughout *The Dispensary;* and if Dryden's influence upon Garth was less extensive than Boileau's, it was nevertheless of fundamental importance in helping to shape Garth's poetic practice and his approach to the evolving concept of the mock-epic genre.

CHAPTER 3

The Dispensary *as a Poem*

IN his "Life of Garth," Samuel Johnson ascribes much of *The Dispensary*'s success to its laudable moral stance. As Johnson explains: "It was on the side of charity against the intrigues of interest, and of regular learning against licentious usurpation of medical authority, and was therefore naturally favoured by those who read and can judge of poetry."[1] Not all subsequent critics have been so prone to think that the worthiness of Garth's moral theme enhances his poem artistically. For some, the very dignity of that theme makes it unsuitable for the comic purposes of a mock-epic. Thus, in the opinion of W. J. Courthope, "The essence of the mock-heroic is that a trivial subject shall be treated in a magnificent manner. But the building of the Dispensary had a serious object: the controversy excited wide public interest, and there was scarcely anything in the incidents of the quarrel . . . which gave opportunity for comic treatment."[2]

We may readily agree that the moral thesis behind *The Dispensary* (involving, as it does, fundamental questions of charity and compassion) is in itself neither comic nor insignificant. Yet it does not follow that such seriousness will inevitably lessen the discrepancy between "trivial subject" and "magnificent manner" which Courthope rightly considers the *sine qua non* of the mock-heroic. For the "triviality" of Garth's subject does not lie in its ethical implications (which, as in *most* moral satires, are anything but frivolous), but rather in the conspicuously unheroic figures whose personalities and actions the poet depicts. Far from weakening the crucial mock-heroic contrast, the important issues at stake in *The Dispensary* serve to strengthen it by underlining the moral inadequacy of all but a handful of the disputants.

That moral inadequacy becomes most obvious in the pervasive

greed which figures as the ruling passion of almost all of Garth's comic targets. As Garth presents them, the antidispensarians, however disparate otherwise, are alike in possessing an avarice so ingrained that no claims of conscience or public good can stand before it. A historian might well object to the distortion of fact that such a view entails, but for Garth's satiric purposes it has the tactical virtue of dramatic simplicity. By proceeding on the tacit assumption that the proclaimed motives of his enemies are too transparently bogus to require refutation, Garth frees himself to concentrate on delineating the precise dimensions of that instinctive rapacity which makes all the antidispensarians brothers.

Having himself played a prominent and partisan role in the dispensary conflict, Garth stands in a markedly different relationship to his subject than does Boileau to the bickering clerics of *Le Lutrin* or Pope to the belles and beaux of *The Rape of the Lock*. Both Boileau and Pope, as putatively neutral outsiders in the conflicts they describe, can plausibly assume positions of disinterested superiority from which to issue more or less evenhanded ridicule of either side. Garth, on the other hand, can hardly pretend to an above-the-battle detachment, and so he declares his allegiance in the preface, where he explains that ". . . finding the animosities among the members of the college of physicians increasing daily, . . . I was persuaded to attempt something of this nature . . . to endeavour to rally some of the disaffected members into a sense of their duty. . . . If the satire may appear directed at any particular person, it is at such only as are presumed to be engaged in dishonourable confederacies for mean and mercenary ends, against the dignity of their own profession."[3] As the tenor of these remarks suggests, Garth reserves his greatest contempt not for the apothecaries (whose devotion to "mercenary ends" he no doubt thought entirely predictable), but rather for their allies within the ranks of the College of Physicians. Such men, "Who Int'rest prudently to Oaths prefer,"[4] have in Garth's view committed a kind of professional treason that is doubly culpable on the part of men who—unlike the benighted apothecaries—might be expected to know better.

Yet to point out that Garth makes no serious pretense to neutrality in *The Dispensary* is not to say that he altogether eschews the satiric advantages deriving from a stance of authorial "detachment." In one sense, it could be said that a certain degree of Olympianism is inherent in the poem's genre itself, since one effect of a mock-epic perspective is a tendency to trivialize *all* the contending parties. Moreover, though Garth's sympathies are never in doubt, he deliberately minimizes his overt praise for the dispensarians: their moral superiority is conveyed not so much in positive terms as in the contrast offered by the egregious roguery of their opponents. We do not meet the dispensarians at all until the poem is more than two thirds over, and with one or two exceptions (e.g., Machaon, who represents the president of the College of Physicians),[5] they are far from impressive figures—albeit infinitely preferable to their opposite numbers. In the interest of balance Garth even offers an occasional mild satiric thrust at certain of his allies. Thus the dignity of Stentor, who rallies the physicians to fight, is undercut both by his name (Stentor is the most bombastic of the Greeks in *The Iliad*) and his characterization ("True to Extreams, yet to dull Forms a Slave, / He's always dully gay, or vainly grave"—V, 137-38). Likewise in canto 6, when Celsus accompanies the goddess Health to the underworld, one of the spirits he meets is that of his dead mistress, who chides her "guilty Lover" for having abandoned her (VI, 203-11).

Another of Garth's gestures toward evenhandedness is his running joke about how proficient his fellow doctors are at killing patients—almost as proficient, it seems, as their apothecary rivals. Sloth, for example, describes the members of the College of Physicians as "the Homicides of *Warwick-Lane*" (I, 178), and Colon expresses his envy over the professional "Right t'Assasinate" (II, 175) enjoyed by doctors. Perhaps the most informed testimony on this point comes from Charon, who explains to Celsus that physicians are especially appreciated in Hades, since "Our awful Monarch and his Consort owe / To them the Peopl'ing of their Realms below" (VI, 148-49). Such allusions led Steven Phillips to conclude that "Garth, to his credit, does not hesitate to attack the College of Physicians."[6] Yet by way of qualification, it should be noted that Garth's jibes against his fellow dispensarians are comparatively few in number and of a general tone that is (in Phillips's words) "often closer to humor than to rebuke."[7] Ironically, the playfulness of his doctor jokes did not keep some of Garth's more sensitive colleagues from taking offense, which prompted Garth to remark in his preface that "The killing of numbers of patients is so trite a piece of raillery, that it ought not to make the least impression. . . ."[8]

I *Epic Parallels and Characterization*

As befits the author of a mock-epic, Garth seasons his poem with comic imitations of his serious predecessors. Though he follows no single epic prototype closely, in spirit his nearest serious model is *The Iliad,* whose theme—discord among leaders—is similar to his own. Of the numerous epic analogues in *The Dispensary,* the majority are relatively generalized—i.e., parodic versions of epic techniques, conventions, or mannerisms not clearly ascribable to any one original. Instances of more specific parallels are not lacking, however, and a few representative examples may serve to indicate the nature of Garth's epic adaptations. Thus, Homer's elaborate description of Achilles' shield in *The Iliad* (book 18) is closely parodied in Garth's description of Querpo's shield (canto 5), and young Querpoïdes reacts to his father's armor (canto 5) in much the same way as Hector's son, Astyanax, does in Homer's epic (book 6). Similarly, the language in which Garth depicts the initial attack of the apothecaries (canto 5) is a comic version of that applied to the charging Trojans in *The Iliad* (book 3).

Garth's single most sizable borrowing from an epic model is the visit to the underworld, which occupies the bulk of canto 6. For this journey Garth owes an obvious debt (which he twice acknowledges in footnotes) to book 6 of *The Aeneid* and Vergil's account of his hero's descent into the nether regions. Both in its general outline and in certain of its details (e.g., the use of a guide and the stops made along the way to interview the dead) Garth's version parallels Vergil's. *The Aeneid* (perhaps via *Le Lutrin*) is also Garth's source for such incidents as Horoscope's sleepless night in canto 3, which in language and spirit draws heavily upon the distracted Dido's insomnia in book 4 of Vergil's epic. Again, for the building of Horoscope's sacrificial altar to Disease (canto 3), Garth adapts for comic purposes many details from the account of Dido's funeral pyre (book 4).[9] To any list of Garth's epic borrowings should also be added his use of a source nearer to home—Milton's *Paradise Lost.* The closest Miltonic echoes come in canto 3 of *The Dispensary,* where the formal series of harangues before the assembled apothecaries is clearly modeled on the great council in Hell, as given in book 2 of Milton's poem. Similarly, Satan's journey through Chaos (book 2) furnishes Garth with verbal and pictorial details for Horoscope's journey to the Fortunate Isles (canto 4).

For all his reliance on the classical epic, when it comes to the supernatural "machinery" of *The Dispensary* Garth does not follow the example of Homer, Vergil, or Milton. Instead, as with so much else, he takes his lead from Boileau, and in place of the customary deities from mythology, he uses a series of allegorical personifications as the principle nonhuman figures in his poem. Like the gods and goddesses who loom so large in the ancient epic, Garth's Sloth, Envy, Disease, Discord, and Health are central to the action. They instigate the conflict, rally the opposing factions, and interpose (both directly and in disguise) at crucial moments in the developing action.[10]

In Garth's own day, the machinery of *The Dispensary* was accorded particular praise by Samuel Wesley, who, in *An Epistle to a Friend Concerning Poetry* (1700), asserts that *"G[art]h, tho barren is his Theme and mean,* / By this [i.e., the machinery] has *reach'd* at least the famed *Lutrine."*[11] More equivocally, Addison, while discussing the suitability of personifications in the epic *(The Spectator,* No. 273), points out that "We find in Mock-Heroic Poems, particularly in the *Dispensary* and the *Lutrin,* several Allegorical Persons of this Nature, which are very beautiful in those Compositions, and may, perhaps, be used as an Argument, that the Authors of them were of Opinion, such Characters might have a Place in an Epic work."[12] But Garth's personified abstractions—which by their very natures tend to be relatively faceless and unindividualized—have not found favor with modern critics, most of whom agree with Richmond Bond, that "the allegorical machinery [of *The Dispensary*] is uninteresting. . . ."[13] Without necessarily rejecting that opinion, we may note that for Garth's purposes, the very stereotyping inherent in allegorical personifications has the advantage of efficiently conveying immediate characterization. A figure introduced to us as Sloth or as Envy has, in effect, been fully characterized just by being named, and though Garth may go on to elaborate upon that characterization with further description or dialogue, he need not spend much time establishing the elementary fact of Sloth's laziness or of Discord's contentiousness.

It is not only the allegorical figures in *The Dispensary* that assume a generic quality; even Garth's human characters, although many are based upon specific persons, have a way of coming through less as idiosyncratic individuals than as broadly representative personality types.[14] Like the Theophrastan prose "Characters" popularized earlier in the century by Sir Thomas Overbury and Joseph Hall, Garth's human figures are essentially defined by one or two obsessive personality traits which dominate their words and actions. Thus, in Horoscope we may detect the outlines of "An Avaricious Man," or in Colocynthis those of "A Vainglorious Warrior." Another, but analogous, literary ancestry is suggested in those speeches wherein Garth's characters, like the personified vices in a medieval morality play, reveal themselves by straightforwardly confessing to or (more often) boasting about their ruling passions. Typically, we find Mirmillo proclaiming:

> Long have I reign'd unrival'd in the Town,
> Glutted with Fees, and mighty in Renown.
> There's none can dye with due Solemnity,
> Unless his Pass-port first be sign'd by Me.
> My arbitrary Bounty's undeny'd,
> I give Reversions, and for Heirs provide.
> None cou'd the tedious Nuptial State support,
> But I, to make it easie, make it short.
>
> (V, 11-18)

Since it is the antidispensarian forces who dominate the poem and since Garth views those forces as motivated almost exclusively by greed, it is inevitable that Garth's satiric portraits show a certain sameness. Naturally, Garth includes a good deal of subsidiary detail whereby such individual qualities as Colon's self-importance, Diasenna's cowardice, or Horoscope's superstition are brought to the fore. However, since such distinctions seem minor in comparison to the overriding acquisitive zeal these characters have in common, there is some justice in Johnson's complaint that "Garth exhibits no discrimination of characters, and . . . what any one says might with equal propriety have been said by another."[15]

For all the strong family resemblance in most of Garth's adverse characters, there are at least a few portraits in *The Dispensary* of a more distinctly personalized cast. It was, in fact,

Garth's satiric portraits of recognizable persons that led John Dennis to classify the poem among the "Libels, which have pass'd for Satires. . . . They are indeed, if you please, beautiful Libels, but they are every where full of Flattery or Slander, and a just Satire admits of neither. . . . The business of Sir *Samuel Garth* in his *Dispensary* was to expose much better Physicians than himself, for no other reason but because they were not of his Opinion in the affair of the *Dispensary*."[16] While we need not necessarily accept Dennis's jaundiced view of Garth's motives, it is obvious that some degree of animus does lie behind the poem's relative handful of closely individualized characterizations. Since Garth felt so much more indignation toward the dissident members of the College of Physicians than toward the lowly apothecaries, it is his portraits of the "Apothecaries Physicians" that are most personalized and therefore the most satirically barbed. If, for example, we examine the portrait of Horoscope, leader of the apothecaries, we find him portrayed less as a particular person than as the epitome of a greedy quack—hence the uncertainty as to his original.[17] On the other hand, the individualized descriptions of such antidispensarian physicians as Querpo (IV, 97-105), Carus (IV, 106-37), Umbra (IV, 138-49), and the Bard (IV, 171-91) leave little room for doubt as to Garth's real-life targets.

The descriptive names Garth assigns to his *dramatis personae* play an important, if obvious, role in their characterization. The dispensarians are mostly given appropriately complimentary names drawn from history or literature. Thus, Machaon and Stentor are heroes from *The Iliad*; Chiron is the medical tutor of Aesculapius in Ovid's *Metamorphoses*; and Celsus is named for A. Cornelius Celsus, author of a first-century A.D. medical encyclopedia. For his comic characters Garth also sometimes turns to a classical source, as in the case of Vagellius (lawyer to the apothecaries), who is named after a character in Juvenal's satires. More frequently, however, Garth gives his antidispensarians names descriptively appropriate to their personalities. In this way, Horoscope's name suggests his superstition; Umbra (literally "shadow") is suitably insubstantial; and Carus (a medical term for "coma") is naturally torpid. One of Garth's favorite ways of naming his characters is to draw upon the terminology of disease and its treatment, with special attention to the scatological. To this category belong such names as Colon (the lower digestive tract), Diasenna and Colocynthis (both powerful purgatives), Ascarides (a rectal parasite), and Giacum (a plant used in treating syphilis).

Perhaps the weakest aspect of Garth's characterization is his willingness to violate a character's consistency in order to convey some immediate comic or didactic point. In the speeches of Garth's major personages it is not uncommon to come across sentiments which, though unremarkable in themselves, seem incongruous in the light of the speaker's character. Thus, it is a little disconcerting to find Envy offering a panegyric of Queen Anne (*T.N.*, 731) or the Elder Ascarides expatiating without any detectable irony on the importance of honor (*T.N.*, 736). Somewhat less blatant is the case of Diasenna, who in the course of an address to his fellow apothecaries, nostalgically recalls "those golden Days of old" (III, 143) when the only rivalry between physicians and apothecaries was to see "Who best cou'd fill his Purse, and thin the Town" (III, 132). In those halcyon times, as he puts it,

> . . . Priests increas'd, and Piety decay'd,
> Churchmen the Church's Purity betray'd;
> Their Lives and Doctrine Slaves and Atheists made.
> The Laws were but the hireling Judge's Sense;
> Juries were sway'd by venal Evidence.
> Fools were promoted to the Council-Board,
> Tools to the Bench, and Bullies to the Sword.
> Pensions in private were the Senate's Aim;
> And Patriots for a place abandon'd Fame.
>
> (*T.N.*, 735)

In this speech, as in others, Garth sacrifices character consistency by intruding too obviously his own standard of values. Diasenna is in character, satirically speaking, as he glowingly describes the good old days when patients could be killed with impunity. But when he goes on to elaborate that description from the viewpoint (and with the terminology) of a moralist, it is clearly not the avaricious apothecary who is speaking, but rather Garth himself.

Similarly, in the speech which follows Diasenna's, we find another instance of Garth's failure to sustain a character's comic point of view. Colocynthis begins his speech with some disparaging comments about Diasenna's medical skills:

> Thou Scandal of the mighty *Paean*'s Art,
> At thy approach, the Springs of Nature start,
> The Nerves unbrace: Nay, at the sight of thee,
> A Scratch turns Cancer, th'Itch a Leprosie.
>
> (III, 159-62)

Yet immediately after these censorious remarks on his colleague's incompetence, Colocynthis goes on to boast complacently of himself as one of "the *Friends* o' Fates, / Who fill *Church-yards*, and who unpeople States" (III, 163-64). Under the circumstances, it is all the more perplexing to find Colocynthis ending his speech with a series of somber philosophical reflections upon death and immortality (*T.N.*, 736).

The charge of incongruity between character and sentiment was one of the earliest leveled against *The Dispensary*. In his preface to the second edition, Garth refers to "the cavils of some furious critics" whose "grand objection is, that the fury Disease is an improper machine to recite characters. . . ." The allusion is to canto 4, where Disease, roused by the Bard's recitation of his clumsy verses, lectures him on the rules of good poetry and urges him to emulate the examples of Wycherley, Congreve, Dryden, Addison, and others. To those who thought Disease was an unseemly vehicle for seriously intended literary criticism, Garth replied that ". . . though I had the authority of some Greek and Latin poets, upon parallel instances, to justify the design; yet that I might not introduce any thing that seemed inconsistent, or hard, I started this objection myself, to a gentleman, very remarkable in this sort of criticism, who would by no means allow that the contrivance was forced, or the conduct incongruous."[18] This explanation did not satisfy critics like Joseph Warton, who continued to find Garth "guilty of a strange impropriety, which cannot be excused, in making the fury DISEASE talk like a critic, give rules of writing, and a panegyric on the best poets of the age."[19]

II *"The Union of Contraries"*

While inconsistencies in Garth's characterization may be counted a serious flaw, a different sort of incongruity—this time as applied to metaphor—is one of his most felicitous satiric devices. This noteworthy feature of Garth's imagery and allusion is seen in his mixture of the heroic and the ridiculous, whereby he emphasizes the difference between the two by acting as if oblivious to it. One of the "original elements" Geoffrey Tillotson credits to Garth is precisely "the method of laying down parallel stripes of the beautiful and the sordid, of enforcing his scale of values by pretending not to have one."[20] A typical example of this approach is found in Garth's description of the arrival of the dawn:

> With that, a Glance from mild *Aurora*'s Eyes,
> Shoots thro' the Crystal Kingdoms of the Skies;
> The Savage Kind in Forests cease to roam,
> And Sots o'ercharg'd with nauseous Loads reel home.
> Light's chearful Smiles o'er th'Azure Waste are spread,
> And Miss from Inns o'Court bolts out unpaid.
>
> (III, 51-56)

It was Garth's use of this technique that Pope imitated (and improved upon) in such lines as those in which Ariel, conjecturing as to the nature of the disaster approaching Belinda, juxtaposes the serious and the trivial—i.e., "Whether the Nymph shall break *Diana*'s Law, / Or some frail *China* Jar receive a Flaw" etc. (*The Rape of the Lock*, II, 105ff.).

Given the nature of his subject matter and his profession, it is only natural that Garth should fill his poem with images drawn from the world of medicine. In *The Philosophy of Rhetoric* (1776), George Campbell cites this aspect of *The Dispensary*; to illustrate poetic wit based on "queerness or singularity of the imagery," Campbell quotes the lines:

> Then *Hydrops* next appears amongst the *Throng*;
> Bloated, and big, she slowly sails along.
> But, like a Miser, in Excess she's poor;
> And pines for Thirst amidst her wat'ry Store.
>
> (VI, 122-25)

Campbell remarks: "The wit in these lines doth not so much arise from the comparison they contain of the dropsy to a miser . . . as from the union of contraries they present to the imagination, poverty in the midst of opulence, and thirst in one who is already drenched in water."[21]

Aside from furnishing him with dramatic similitudes like these, Garth's medical imagery proved to be eminently adaptable to the special deflationary ends of the mock-epic. So much of medical practice involves the earthy, the squalid, and the malodorous that Garth is able to draw upon an all but inexhaustible supply of reductive allusions and comic associations. As might be expected from the scatalogical names he so often assigned his characters, Garth's medical imagery leans heavily upon the excretory and the indelicate. Thus, when Horoscope faints, his servant revives him with the contents of a urinal (II, 206-7). Similarly, Carus' claims to cure lunacy remind Garth that ". . . when Perfumes their fragrant Scent give o're / Nought can their Odour, like a Jakes, restore" (IV, 114-15). And prominent among the symbolic designs on Querpo's shield is a representation of "*Leeches* spouting *Hemorrhoidal* Blood" (V, 106). Such allusions (of which many more could be given) reach their culmination in canto 5 when the opposing forces meet in a battle whose weapons consist largely of syringes, chamber pots, bed pans, and a variety of emetic and purgative drugs.

It is not only by means of toilet humor that Garth creates what Arthur Murphy commends as the "many beautiful Passages in his *Dispensary*, where a Ridicule is thrown upon his Heroes by associating with them Images of Things, to which some Kind of Turpitude is adherent."[22] Almost as numerous as Garth's references to matters digestive are his allusions to the related topic of sexual mischance. We learn, for example, that the murals in the Apothecaries' Hall deal in such subjects as techniques of abortion, the restoration of virility, and the curing of venereal disease (III, 115-22). Likewise, we are told that Mirmillo, who specializes in treating gonorrhea and syphilis (IV, 29-33), recruits most of his patients from among the "Country Dames" who "find a Spark, and after lose a Nose" (IV, 25-26). When the battle is joined in canto 5, prominent among the antidispensarian warriors is Siphilus, whose "maim'd Fore-head" is disfigured by the "scaly Crusts" (V, 194) symptomatic of his malady. Significantly, almost all of the pathetic group of representative patients assembled in Horoscope's waiting room (II, 127-48) are on some sexually connected quest, whether for a love potion, an abortion, a fertility drug, a beauty restorative, a venereal cure, or an aphrodisiac.

III "Admired and Elegant Reflections"

Offensive as Garth's medico-scatology might be to the squeamish, in the antiheroic world of his poem it is both thematically appropriate and satirically effective. As Garth was well aware, however, an unrelieved emphasis on physical and moral squalor can easily become oppressive; and so he has included in *The Dispensary* a considerable amount of material consciously designed to add to the poem's dignity and to alleviate the otherwise sordid atmosphere. Such material—consisting mostly of poetic descriptions, philosophical reflections, and moral sententiae—is interspersed throughout the work, and though such passages are usually brief, in at least two instances (the journey to the Fortunate Islands in canto 4 and the trip to the Elysian Fields in canto 6) the serious note is sustained at some length.

Illustrative of Garth's nonsatiric embellishments are such passages as the description of nightfall:

> The Ev'ning now with blushes warms the Air,
> The Steer resigns his Yoke, the Hind his Care.
> The Clouds aloft with golden Edgings glow,
> And falling Dews refresh the Flow'rs below.
> The Bat with sooty wings flits thro' the Grove,
> The Reeds scarce rustle, nor the Aspine move,
> And all the feather'd Folks forbear their Lays of Love.
>
> (*T.N.*, 738)

Or the description of the creatures hibernating in the "Chambers of the Globe":

> The Insects here their lingring Trance survive:
> Benumn'd they seem, and doubtful if alive.
> From Winter's fury hither they repair,
> And stay for milder Skies and softer Air.
> Down to these Cells obscener Reptils creep,
> Where hateful *Nutes* and painted *Lizzards* sleep.
> Where shiv'ring *Snakes* the Summer Solstice wait;
> Unfurl their painted Folds, and slide in State.
>
> (VI, 52-59)

To these examples may be added the lines (once among the most admired in the poem) on death:

> To Die, is Landing on some silent Shoar,
> Where Billows never break, nor Tempests roar;
> E'er well we feel the friendly Stoke, 'tis o're.
> The Wise thro' Thought th'Insults of Death defy;
> The Fools, thro' bless'd insensibility.
> 'Tis what the Guilty fear, the Pious crave;
> Sought by the Wretch, and vanquish'd by the Brave.
> It eases Lovers, sets the Captives free;
> And, tho' a Tyrant, offers Liberty.
>
> (*T.N.*, 736)

The heavy use of such material has been criticized by Ian Jack, who feels that Garth's "passages of picturesque natural description . . . stand out as excrescenses"[23] in the poem; and it is true enough that Garth's descriptive and philosophical vignettes, however well done in themselves, can sometimes strike a discordant note. This is especially apt to occur in those cases where the passage is so protracted as to vitiate the satiric tone of the poem or where (as pointed out earlier) a seriously intended homiletic message is placed in the mouth of an otherwise farcical character. It is also true that Garth's more formal excursions sometimes show a self-conscious striving for the "sublime," which for many modern readers weakens the verse by giving it an intrusive air of "artificiality."[24] And finally, Garth's longer passages of descriptive and philosophical ornamentation may be fairly charged with impeding the dramatic action of his poem.[25]

It is indicative of how much poetic tastes have changed that the very passages of luxuriant description and lofty reflection which present-day readers are apt to see as flaws in *The Dispensary* were among those most often selected for special praise by Garth's contemporaries. It was as much for its "elevated sense" as for its satiric vigor that Thomas Cheek commended *The Dispensary* in his dedicatory poem,[26] just as the anonymous author of a letter to *Mist's Weekly Journal* (June 8, 1728) thought it natural to speak of the "admired and elegant reflections which are the Beauties of Garth."[27] So well-received were Garth's more mellifluous passages that when Edward Bysshe published what his subtitle described as a "Collection of the most Natural, Agreeable and Sublime Thoughts . . . to be found in the best English Poets,"[28] he drew upon *The Dispensary* for no fewer than 468 lines, amounting to one fourth of the entire poem.

IV The "Manly Beauty of Each Nervous Line"

It was not merely the elegance of his sentiments that commended Garth's verse to his contemporaries: they were also impressed by his graceful handling of the couplets whereby those sentiments were conveyed. Though personal friendship may have helped elicit Charles Boyle's praise for the "manly beauty of each nervous line"[29] in *The Dispensary*, even so authoritative a judge as Samuel Johnson praised the "strain of smooth and free versification"[30] in the poem. More recently, critics have acknowledged Garth's importance in helping to shape the heroic couplet to the form in which it came to be used through most of the eighteenth century. Building significantly upon the practice of such predecessors as Dryden, Garth's verse is among the first in English to show to full advantage the qualities of balance, antithesis, and symmetry that we associate with the Augustan heroic couplet. As Clark, in his discussion of couplet evolution, puts it: "It is not till we come to Garth's *The Dispensary* . . . that the medial caesura and antithesis, both of lines and half lines, take their place as the almost constant accompaniment of the stopped couplet."[31] And to Saintsbury's praise of *The Dispensary*'s metrics (cited in chapter 2) may be added his opinion that Garth "was the first writer who took the couplet, as Dryden had fashioned it, . . . and displayed it in the form it maintained throughout the eighteenth century. In some respects it may be said that no advance in this peculiar model was ever made on *The Dispensary*. Its best lines are equal to any of Pope's in mere fashion. . . . [Garth's] versification . . . not only long preceded Pope, but also anticipated Addison's happiest effort by some years."[32]

Characteristic of Garth's handling of the couplet are the lines in which Horoscope describes Vagellius, the unprincipled attorney of the apothecaries:

> Since of each Enterprise th'Event's unknown,
> We'll quit the Sword, and hearken to the Gown.
> Nigh lives *Vagellius*, one reputed long,
> For Strength of Lungs, and Pliancy of Tongue.
> Which way He pleases, he can mould a Cause,
> The Worst has Merits, and the Best has Flaws.
> Five Guinea's make a Criminal to Day,
> And ten to Morrow wipe the Stain away.

> What ever he affirms is undeny'd,
> *Milo*'s the Lecher, *Clodius* th'Homicide.
> *Cato* pernicious, *Cataline* a Saint,
> *Orford* suspected, *Duncombe* innocent.
> Let's then to Law, for 'tis by Fate decreed,
> *Vagellius*, and our Mony, shall succeed.
> (IV, 154-67)

This passage, both in its strengths and weaknesses, may fairly stand as a representative specimen of Garth's versification. In it are displayed the metrical smoothness, conversational ease, and clausal balance that Garth, with very few lapses, preserves through *The Dispensary*. Less admirably (but no less characteristically), the passage shows Garth somewhat blunting his point by diffusion and prolixity. His examples of Vagellius's amoralism, though individually witty and appropriate, are so numerous as to preclude the kind of concise, epigrammatic finality that the heroic couplet displays in the hands of Pope. Moreover, the recurring medial caesura and the regularity of what Spence calls Garth's "antithèses perpetuelles"[33] give this passage a metronomic quality that verges on rhythmical monotony.

One notable characteristic of Garth's prosody is his reliance on *gradus* epithets, or words inserted in order to stretch out an otherwise adequate line to full measure. The *gradus* epithet may be seen as superfluous in that its presence is dictated less by any sense requirements than by the mechanical necessity of filling out the metrical pattern. The device is most often found in Garth's descriptive passages, as in the account of the approach to Hades:

> Now *Celsus*, with his glorious Guide, invades
> The silent Region of the fleeting shades,
> Where Rocks and ruful Desarts are descry'd;
> And sullen *Styx* rouls down his lazy Tide.
> (VI, 138-41)

The *gradus* epithets in these lines are respectively "glorious," "silent" (or, alternately, "fleeting"), "ruful," and "sullen" (or "lazy"). Aside from a minimal descriptive function, they contribute little to the meaning of the lines, which without them can be read quite naturally as iambic tetrameter couplets. Saintsbury—in whose view the *gradus* epithet is "perhaps the worst blemish of [heroic couplet] style"[34]—calls Garth's frequent use of this device the single greatest flaw in his verse technique. Against this opinion, however, we may place that of Johnson, who finds that Garth "never slumbers in self-indulgence; his full vigour is always exerted; scarce a line is left unfinished, nor is it easy to find an expression used by constraint, or a thought imperfectly expressed."[35]

Though in his preface to *The Dispensary* Garth modestly disclaims any ambition to win fame as a poet, his professed indifference is belied by the energy he was to expend in revising, augmenting, and polishing his poem over the course of two decades. A good many of these revisions consist of little more than changing a word or phrase in the interest of greater precision or dramatic effect. For example, the embattled Colon, who in the first edition was merely "angry and revengefull" (V, 197), becomes alliteratively "dauntless and disdainfull" in the second. Similarly, we find Garth, like most poets, endlessly trying—by minor alterations of diction, punctuation, and syntax—to improve the smoothness and cadence of his lines. In this way, the first edition's metrically awkward line, "And int'rest then had directed us t'obey" (III, 130), is adjusted in the second edition ("And Interest had taught us to obey"), and again in the sixth ("And Int'rest then had taught us to obey"), until it reaches its final form in the seventh ("And Int'rest then had bid us but obey"). For at least one minor revision, Alexander Pope seems to have been indirectly responsible. In his *Essay on Criticism* (1711) Pope poked fun at poets who used hackneyed rhymes, pointing out that "Where'e'r you find *the cooling Western Breeze,* / In the next Line, it *whispers thro' the Trees.*"[36] It seems likely that it was in response to this allusion that Garth rewrote the opening lines of canto 2. Originally these read: "Soon as with gentle Sighs the ev'ning Breeze / Begun to whisper thro' the murm'ring Trees" (II, 1-2). For the seventh edition (the first to appear after Pope's *Essay*) Garth rewrote the couplet to read: "Soon as the Ev'ning veil'd the Mountains Heads, / And Winds lay hush'd in subterranean Beds."

Beyond such small (though cumulatively significant) revisions, Garth took advantage of successive editions—particularly the sixth in 1706—to enhance his poem with entirely new material. Since Garth seldom deleted lines from the poem, with each new edition *The Dispensary* grew in size, eventually expanding from the 1418 lines of its first appearance to the 1848 lines of the eighth edition—the last published in Garth's lifetime. For the most part, Garth's alterations do not involve structural change; instead they elaborate upon existing speeches or descriptions, fleshing them out with fuller detail, illustration, and analogy. In size these embellishments range from one or two couplets up to such lengthy increments as Carus' formal address and Querpo's response (forty-seven lines) or the added details of battle description (thirty-six lines)—both inserted in the sixth edition. To that same edition Garth added Horoscope's one hundred and thirty-four line journey to the Fortunate Isles—the poem's largest single revision and the only one which offers an entirely new sequence, rather than an embellishment of earlier material.[37]

The quality of Garth's revisions has long been the subject of dispute. Jonathan Richardson reports that "Mr. Pope told me himself 'there was hardly an alteration of the innumerable ones through every edition that was not for the better'. . . . People have been so accustomed to read [*The Dispensary*] over and over, and even to repeat whole passages by heart of the first edition, that their ear could not bear the change, and they thought it was their judgment. We now see fairly, that every edition was for the better."[38] Among more recent critics, Saintsbury has endorsed a similar view, finding that "the alterations [in *The Dispensary*], as is not always the case, [are] almost invariably improvements."[39]

Yet, as Richardson's remarks make clear, some of *The Dispensary*'s admirers have thought Garth's original version weakened, rather than improved by its emendations. Thomas Killigrew's preference for the unrevised poem is apparent in his *Miscellanea Aurea*. Writing shortly after Garth's death, Killigrew envisages the poet's ascension to Parnassus, but pointedly remarks: ". . . that the Book that was carry'd before him was in *Quarto*; which made me suppose it was the first Edition."[40] Similarly, Elijah Fenton (in a letter to William Broome on September 7, 1726) cites Garth's reworkings of this poem as an example of how "Too much handling of verses is apt to wear off the natural gloss. . . ."[41] And Frank Ellis, Garth's modern editor, has agreed with such opinions, explaining that one reason he chose the second edition as his copy-text is that he considers it "a better poem" than the subsequent editions incorporating Garth's major changes. Of these changes, Ellis remarks: "Many . . . are repetitions of situations or turns of phrase already in the poem. Others are clearly adventitious or anachronistic. Still others are merely hackneyed."[42]

A consideration of Garth's revisions of *The Dispensary* on an individual rather than a collective basis suggests that neither the categorical praise by some critics nor the equally categorical disparagement by others is fully justifiable. Though it seems likely that most modern readers would join Ellis in his adverse opinion of Garth's revisions, it is not hard to find instances wherein a speech is considerably enhanced, a description strengthened, or a characterization sharpened by Garth's reworking. Thus, the formal portrait of Urim—which was not added to canto 1 until the sixth edition (*T.N.*, 729)—is not only one of Garth's more accomplished character sketches, but also one which serves to reinforce the satiric point of Sloth's mock-panegyric of lazy clerics. Likewise, the simmering indignation that Diasenna's pacifism arouses in Colocynthis is rendered both more comic and more dramatic by the description (added to the seventh edition) of how

> Sow'r Ferments on his shining Surface swim,
> Work up to Froth and Bubble o'er the Brim:
> Not *Beauties* fret so much if Freckles come,
> Or Nose shou'd redden in the Drawing-Room:
> Or *Lovers* that mistake th'appointed Hour,
> Or in the lucky Minute want the Pow'r.
>
> (*T.N.*, 735)

Unfortunately, such improvements over the original, though by no means rare, are rather less frequent than changes of a more dubious value. A large proportion of Garth's embellishments are of the sententious or picturesquely descriptive variety discussed earlier. As Garth intended, such material does contribute a note of elegance to the otherwise "low" proceedings; yet in practice these additions (especially as they accumulate in the later versions) create a diffuseness that somewhat weakens the poem's comic impact. The lengthy, nonsatiric account of Horoscope's journey to the Fortunate Isles is in itself a commendable performance, but it cannot be said to contribute much to either plot or characterization. Moreover, in context, the whole incident, coming after the concentrated mock-heroics of the war council, seems anticlimactic and dissipative of the comic momentum established earlier in the canto. By the same token, in his revisions Garth tends to indulge in his old weakness for inserting incongruously lofty or serious sentiments in the mouths of otherwise farcical personages. Since Garth seldom deleted material, one cumulative effect of his revisions is a blurring of the poem's satiric focus; and it is that blurring, more than any other single element, which validates Ellis's preference for the uncluttered second edition.

V "Accidental and Extrinsick Popularity"

A prominent factor in the contemporary success of *The Dispensary* was the topicality of its subject and treatment. At the time Garth produced his poem, the long-standing dispute between physicians and apothecaries, however parochial its origins, had become a topic of widespread interest. The enthusiasm with which the literate public greeted what Steele called "Dr. *Garth's* Nine days Wonder"[43] derived at least in part from the pleasure of tracing out its references to living persons and current events. But it is in the nature of such an appeal that, as a work's subject fades in immediacy and interest, the very topicality that was once so enhancing becomes an obstacle to understanding and enjoyment.

That Garth was fully aware of this truism and hoped to minimize the effect is suggested by the character of his revisions, so many of which (as we have seen) are attempts to universalize the poem with such timeless materials as philosophic homilies and descriptive flights. For all Garth's efforts, however, as the dispensary dispute receded into history, the appeal of the poem inevitably diminished with it. By 1767, Oliver Goldsmith remarked that "The praises bestowed upon this poem are more than have been given to any other; but our approbation, at present, is cooler, for it owed part of its fame to party"[44]; and a few years later, Johnson credited some of the poem's initial success to the "accidental and extrinsick popularity"[45] created by its timely subject matter.

Of all the topical allusions in *The Dispensary*, it is ironical that the one which has attracted the most attention (primarily in the form of condemnation) should be a brief, almost perfunctory aside on a matter peripheral to Garth's central concern. The lines in question occur in canto 5 during a speech in which Discord addresses Mirmillo, who has announced his intention to write an antidispensarian tract. Such a work, Discord maintains, would do the cause more harm than good, since dull-witted pamphlets have a way of provoking brilliant rejoinders: "So *Diamonds* take a Lustre from their Foyle;/And to a *Bentley* 'tis, we owe a *Boyle*" (V, 73-74). In the nineteenth century, when so much else about *The Dispensary* had been forgotten, Lord Macaulay still recalled how "Garth insulted Bentley and extolled Boyle in lines which are now never quoted except to be laughed at."[46] No less pejorative is the opinion of R. C. Jebb, who writes that "Garth has pilloried himself for ever by the couplet in which he celebrated Boyle's supposed triumph."[47] And more recently, H. W. Garrod has characterized the same lines as "Garth's preposterous *mot*."[48]

In the couplet which elicited these unflattering remarks, Garth is referring to *The Epistles of Phalaris* debate—itself a relatively minor skirmish in the larger pamphlet war over the ancients-moderns question. To Sir William Temple, the superiority of ancient writers over those more recent seemed obvious; and in his *Essay on Ancient and Modern Learning* (1690) he expounded that view, citing the recently "discovered" manuscript of *The Epistles of Phalaris* (supposedly dating from the sixth century B.C.) as a work whose excellence no latter-day author could ever hope to match. In 1695 an edition of *The Epistles* was published by Charles Boyle, the future fourth earl of Orrery, but at the time still an Oxford undergraduate. In his preface, Boyle lavishly praised Temple and referred disparagingly to Richard Bentley, a formidable scholar who was known to question the authenticity of the Phalaris manuscript. Stung by Boyle's remarks, in 1697 Bentley published a *Dissertation on the Epistles of Phalaris*, wherein he conclusively demonstrated the spuriousness of the Phalaris manuscript and ridiculed Temple and Boyle for having been taken in. Boyle's answer (written with the help of friends) came in *Doctor Bentley's Dissertation Examin'd* (1698), which loftily denounces Bentley for his manners, his prose style, and—with a good deal less conviction—his scholarship.[49] As the derisive comments on Garth's couplet suggest, posterity has so thoroughly vindicated Bentley in this exchange that Garth's praise of Boyle has come to seem absurd.

In Garth's defense, it is only fair to point out that his view of the matter, however mistaken it may appear in retrospect, was the overwhelmingly dominant one in the literary society of his day. Throughout *The Epistles of Phalaris* debate (and, indeed, the entire ancients-moderns controversy) there is a distinct undercurrent of class antagonism. To the proponents of the ancients, a man like Bentley—with his grim professionalism and his graceless prose style—seemed to epitomize a growing bourgeois threat to the gentlemanly traditions of taste and good-breeding in literature. For many in the polite literary world of the late seventeenth century, the fact that Bentley happened to be right about *The Epistles of Phalaris* was far less important than the inherent unseemliness of his attacks on the aristocratic Temple and Boyle. Over and over again in contemporary allusions to Bentley, we find him pictured as a boorish, uncultivated, and ill-bred pedant whose attempts to correct his social and cultural betters are by definition presumptuous.[50]

In the light of Garth's literary sympathies, it is only natural to find him sharing this view. In a general sense, the ancients-moderns controversy may even be said to resemble the physicians-apothecaries dispute, in that both involve a traditional elite being challenged by those it considered to be its inferiors in both learning and genealogy. Thus Boyle, in his commendatory verse on *The Dispensary*, praised Garth for the way his

> . . . pointed satire's sterling wit,
> Does only knaves or formal blockheads hit;
> Who're gravely dull, insipidly serene,
> And carry all their wisdom in their mien;
> Whom thus expos'd, thus stripp'd of their disguise,
> None will again admire, most will despise![51]

Appropriately enough, Boyle's sneers at the antidispensarians are substantially similar in tone to the insults he and his supporters regularly directed against Bentley.

A further aspect of Garth's topicality in *The Dispensary* that deserves mention is his use of panegyric. As a satirist, Garth is naturally more concerned with castigating his enemies than with praising his heroes, and so for the most part his complimentary allusions to specific persons are brief, consisting of little more than a commendatory phrase or two. A notable exception, however, is made for Garth's greatest personal hero, King William III, who is the recipient not only of numerous flattering references, but also of two extended formal tributes (I, 137-54; VI, 275-98).[52] Garth had already flatteringly celebrated William in the Harveian Oration (1697), and in *The Dispensary* he strikes a similar note of adulation. Illustrative of Garth's compliments to William are the remarks which the ghost of Harvey addresses to the College of Physicians:

> Then *Naussau's* Health shall be your glorious Aim,
> He shou'd be as Immortal as his Name.
> Some Princes Claims from Devastation spring:
> He condescends in pity to be King:
> And when, amidst his *Olives* plac'd, He stands,
> And governs more by Candour than Commands:
> Ev'n then not less a Heroe he appears,
> Than when his *Laurel* Diadem he wears.
>   Wou'd but *Apollo* some great Bard inspire
> With sacred veh'mence of Poetick Fire;
> To celebrate in Song that God-like Power,
> Which did the labouring Universe restore;
> Fair *Albion's* Cliffs wou'd Eccho to the Strain,
> And praise the Arm that Conquer'd to regain
> The Earth's repose, and Empire o'er the Main.
>   (VI, 275-89)

As we might expect, the reactions of Garth's contemporaries to such encomia were as much dictated by political sympathies as by critical judgment. Thus, the anonymous Whig author of *The Dissertator in Burlesque* (1701) particularly commends Garth for the way he "Sings / The praises of the best of Kings."[53] On the other hand, Sir Richard Blackmore, in *A Satyr Against Wit* (1699), contemptuously dismisses "*Garth's* Lampoon" as a work "with little in't but Praise"[54]—a rather odd characterization from one who had himself been conspicuously ridiculed in the poem. A more detached (though not necessarily disinterested) opinion is that of Abbé François Leblanc, who in *Letters on the English and French Nations* (1747) writes: "You see, the English poets are to blame, in charging ours with flattery, as a vice peculiar to them. Perhaps the celebrated Dryden, Rowe, Addison, and Dr. Garth, have carried it farther, than any writer of what nation soever. Notwithstanding the praise the English bestow on this last author, on account of his *Dispensary*, which is only an imitation of the *Lutrin*, he has not surpassed Boileau except in exaggerating the praises he has copied from him to celebrate King William."[55] In our own day, Bond has written that Garth's "panegyric on the King mar[s] the burlesque" of *The Dispensary*;[56] and Karlernst Schmidt, echoing LeBlanc's contention that Garth's flattery is more fulsome than Boileau's, remarks: "Was bei Boileau als Vorsichtsmassregel und Konvention interpretiert werden kann, hat bei Garth den Anschein einer durch das Vorbild ermutigten echten Begeisterung"[57] ("What can be read in Boileau as a protective measure and convention, has in Garth the appearance of a genuine enthusiasm inspired by his model").

As Schmidt's remarks suggest, there is little doubt that Garth's primary motive in extolling King William was a perfectly sincere admiration for a monarch most Whigs viewed as England's savior. Beyond such considerations, however, it seems likely that Garth meant his panegyrics to perform a valid artistic function in the poem: for though satire naturally stresses the negative aspects of its subject matter, to be fully effective a satirist must inform us not only of what he dislikes, but also of what he admires—since it is only when we are aware of an author's positive standards that we can adequately gauge the folly or perfidy of those who violate them. In a mock-epic, the ideal against which the satiric targets are to be measured is largely implicit in the heroic associations evoked by the genre itself. But Garth (in keeping with his metaphor on Boyle and Bentley) evidently thought that a more immediate and explicit model of heroic virtue might be useful to point up the moral and mental failures of the antidispensarians. That the two panegyrics of King William are intended to perform such a function is suggested by the positions they occupy in the poem: in effect, they serve as a kind of prologue and epilogue—one occurring early in the first canto as the action begins, and the other appearing at the end of the sixth and concluding canto.

Ironically, Garth's poem might have been better served had his admiration for William been less heartfelt; for it is the very fervor of his esteem that betrays Garth into the extravagance so many readers have found objectionable. Yet, in Garth's own time, as we have seen, there were those who thought the glowing panegyrics of William especially commendable. Indeed, Henry

Blount called upon Garth to undertake an even more ambitious poetic celebration of the king:

> Now let your Muse rise with expanded wings,
> To sing the fate of empires and of kings;
> Great William's victories she'll next rehearse,
> And raise a trophy of immortal verse:
> Thus to your art proportion the design,
> And mighty things with mighty numbers join,
> A second Namur, or a future Boyne.[58]

Despite the congeniality of the proposed subject, Garth declined the proferred advice, and was content to let *The Dispensary* stand as his foremost claim for admission to Parnassus.

CHAPTER 4

The Other Works

IN 1709, after remarking on Garth's literary inactivity since his poetic debut, William Coward ironically commended his friend's restraint:

> In this the *Dispensarian Poet's* wise.
> *Once* he wrote well, and lets that *once* suffice:
> Provokes no *Critics* in a second Muse,
> Establish'd Fame, by *new Attempts* to lose.[1]

Although Garth's pen had by no means been as idle as Coward's lines suggest, it is true that in the decade immediately following publication of *The Dispensary* Garth's literary efforts were limited to a relative handful of translations, occasional verses, and theatrical prologues. As might have been expected from one who in the preface to *The Dispensary* called poetry "an amusement I have very little practised hitherto, nor perhaps ever shall again,"[2] Garth was not a man to allow the claims of authorship precedence over his growing professional, social, and political concerns. Yet, if Garth was never to be a prolific writer, neither was he ever to abandon literature, and in his later years he not only produced a small body of occasional poems, but also undertook works of a more ambitious nature, such as *Claremont* (1715) and the translation of Ovid's *Metamorphoses* (1717)—both of which significantly enhanced the literary reputation he had earned with *The Dispensary*.

I Claremont

Among the other literary news that John Gay included in his letter to William Congreve on April 7, 1715, was word that "Sir Samuel Garth's Poem upon my Lord Clare's house I believe will be published in the Easter-Week."[3] On May 2 the poem duly appeared, printed by Tonson as a handsome folio and formally addressed to Thomas Pelham-Holles (1693-1768), the wealthy young nobleman whose recently acquired country estate it commemorates. Garth's first acquaintance with Pelham-Holles seems to have come through the Kit-Cat Club, and by 1714, when Pelham-Holles was created earl of Clare, he had become important in Garth's life as a personal friend, a sometime patient, and a valuable patron.[4] Shortly after receiving his earldom, Clare purchased from Sir John Vanbrugh a small parcel of land near Esher in Surrey where Vanbrugh had earlier built himself a modest house. After enlarging the estate by land purchases, Clare commissioned Vanbrugh to design and build for him a palatial country home to be named "Claremont." In 1715, as the house was nearing completion, Garth composed his poem.

In form *Claremont* belongs to the genre of the "place" poem (alternately the "topographical" or "local" poem), defined by Johnson as a work "of which the fundamental subject is some particular landscape to be poetically described, with the addition of such embellishments as may be supplied by historical retrospection or incidental meditation."[5] As it developed in England during the seventeenth and eighteenth centuries, the form reflected certain elements from the works of Vergil and Ovid. To Vergil (primarily in the *Eclogues*) may be traced the tradition from which the "place" poem derives its customary descriptions of pastoral simplicity and virtue (see *Claremont,* ll. 88-159).[6] Likewise, it is ultimately to Vergil's *Georgics* (from which Garth takes his epigraph) that the "place" poem owes its emphasis upon didactic nature lore—as, for example, in *Claremont's* explication of Druidic meteorology (ll. 160-69). Equally pervasive in the "place" poem is the influence of Ovid, whose *Metamorphoses* furnished prototypes for the naiads, fauns, and nymphs who figure so largely in such works. Thus, the tale of Montano, which Garth places at the center of *Claremont,* is a straightforward recasting of the Narcissus and Echo story from book 3 of the *Metamorphoses.*

In his preface Garth acknowledges two contemporary works whose influence on *Claremont* was formative: "They that have seen those two excellent poems of Cooper's-hill and Windsor-forest; the one by sir J. Denham, the other by Mr. Pope; will show a great deal of candour if they approve of this."[7] Denham's

Cooper's Hill (1642) is generally credited with starting in England the fashion for poems which describe a geographic location, narrate its real and legendary past, and set forth whatever political, social, and moral lessons the poet thinks appropriate. Of the numerous "place" poems *Cooper's Hill* helped inspire, the most accomplished was Pope's *Windsor Forest* (1713), published only two years before *Claremont*—though parts of Pope's poem were composed as early as 1704, and Garth may well have seen these in manuscript. To such predecessors Garth owes his theme, his general approach, and certain of his specific techniques. Yet *Claremont,* though derivative, is by no means a simple exercise in imitation, and within the confines of the "place" poem tradition, Garth has shaped a work that bears his personal stamp.

The 329 lines of *Claremont* fall naturally into five divisions of differing length, subject matter, and emphasis. The opening section (ll. 1-46) contains a denunciation of adulatory poets and their fatuous patrons; this is followed by a section (ll. 47-87) in which Lord Clare is offered as an example of deserved praise and his estate is briefly described; in the third portion of the poem (ll. 88-204) we are taken back to ancient Britain and the Druids, whose pastoral simplicity is contrasted to modern decadence; the fourth section (ll. 205-98) tells the story of Montano and Echo (whose tragedy is enacted on the future site of Claremont); and the fifth and concluding section of the poem (ll. 299-329) offers a prophecy by Druid priests of the coming reign of George I.

In the very first lines of *Claremont,* Garth, foregoing any invocation of the Muse, goes directly to a satiric survey of the contemporary literary scene, in which he finds ". . . a frenzy has of late possess'd the brain! / Though few can write, yet fewer can refrain" (ll. 1-2). The resultant plague of bad verse, however, cannot be blamed entirely on the poets, for they are sustained and encouraged in their folly by the insatiable vanity of those "Who have a pension or a place to give" (l. 10). Lamentably, "No Muse is proof against a golden shower" (l. 14), and since most patrons reward only the grossest flatterers, it is not surprising to find swarms of venal poets ready to oblige.

> I hate such mercenaries, and would try
> From this reproach to rescue poetry.

> Apollo's sons should scorn the servile art,
> And to court-preachers leave the fulsome part.
>
> (ll. 43-46)

By virtue of its conspicuous position, Garth's pointed condemnation of literary toadyism sets an initial tone rather more acerbic than that found in most "place" poems. Morally speaking, Garth's scorn for fawning poets is an altogether praiseworthy (if unexceptional) sentiment, and there is no reason to question his sincerity in espousing it. From a practical viewpoint, however, it is clear that these lines owe their prominence less to their author's depth of conviction than to his sense of rhetorical strategy. For Garth, borrowing a time-honored tactic, uses his attack on lying panegyrists to lay the groundwork for the "truthful" eulogy of Lord Clare that is to follow. By forcefully announcing his disdain for sycophants, Garth hopes to render less plausible any such charges against himself.

The second section of *Claremont* is marked by the brief appearance of an *adversarius*, who objects to Garth's previous remarks as overly categorical. "What then," Garth imagines being asked, "Must no true sterling pass, / Because impure alloys some coin debase?" (ll. 47-48). Garth readily admits that great men of real merit deserve to be celebrated, in support of which he offers an example of just such a one:

> The man who's honest, open, and a friend,
> Glad to oblige, uneasy to offend;
> Forgiving others, to himself severe;
> Though earnest, easy; civil, yet sincere;
> Who seldom but through great good-nature errs;
> Detesting fraud as much as flatterers;
> 'Tis he my Muse's homage should receive;
> If I could write, or Holles could forgive.
>
> (ll. 51-58)

For all his careful efforts to avoid an appearance of obsequiousness, Garth's generous tribute to Lord Clare may strike many readers as not very different from the kind of puffery he had earlier decried. Yet such a response, though not wholly invalid, would be unfair to Garth; for it overlooks the social and literary context in which he wrote. As Garth's own strictures on the subject indicate, fulsome praise addressed to noblemen was an almost invariable practice among the poets of his day, and while the hope of reward was doubtless a common denominator behind such encomia, it could hardly have been for Garth the only, or even the most important motive. There is ample reason to believe that Garth not only admired Clare as a man, but felt an even greater reverence for the hierarchical tradition he embodied. Along with most Englishmen of his time, Garth fully accepted the principle stated elsewhere in *Claremont* as "None but the virtuous are of noble blood" (l. 319). We should also remember that the poetic eulogist, like the epitaph writer, is engaged in an exercise where scrupulous honesty would be highly inappropriate: a judiciously balanced panegyric would be a contradiction in terms. Moreover, Garth's compliments to Clare, if compared to contemporary analogues (e.g., Dryden's rhapsodic dedications), seem far from hyperbolical. We may take it as a sign of Garth's moderation that he was content to picture Clare merely as a man of excellent character, and not as the godlike paragon we meet two years later in Laurence Eusden's "Poem on the Marriage of His Grace the Duke of Newcastle" (1717).

With his compliments delivered, Garth goes on to describe the arcadian beauties of Clare's new estate and to anticipate the splendors of the noble mansion under construction. The estate having been christened "Claremont," Garth announces that his purpose in the poem will be to explain how ". . . Fame / R`cords from whence the villa took its name" (ll. 86-87). That name, as will emerge from Garth's fanciful etymology, is not the new coinage we might have thought, but rather a title conferred in antiquity and bearing a number of highly romantic associations.

In the third section of *Claremont* Garth takes us back to "times of old" and the ancient Britons, whose honesty and simplicity he contrasts to current moral corruption. Thus we are informed that the women then were strangers to vanity ("No shape-smith set up shop, and drove a trade / To mend the work wise Providence had made"—ll. 98-99); and the men had not yet learned to dissemble ("Upright in actions, and in thought sincere; / And strictly were the same they would appear"—ll. 106-7). Unlike their descendants, these worthy people led lives of wholesome temperance ("No cook with art increas'd physicians' fees, / Nor serv'd up Death in soups and fricasees"—ll. 114-15). Presiding over this admirable society were the Druid priests, of whom Garth tells us:

> Good rules in mild persuasions they convey'd;
> Their lives confirming what their lectures said.
> None violated truth, invaded right;
> Yet had few laws, but will and appetite.
> The people's peace they studied, and profest
> No politics but public interest.
> Hard was their lodging, homely was their food;
> For all their luxury was doing good.
>
> (ll. 142-49)

In his nostalgic description of "those good days of innocence" (l. 124), Garth speaks in the authentic voice of Augustan pastoralism. Few themes are more widespread in European literature than the harking back to an earlier "Golden Age," usually bucolic and always superior in virtue to the present; the tradition was already ancient when Vergil gave it full expression in his *Eclogues* and elsewhere. By Garth's time in England, it was most often the Druids to whom the poets turned when their work required a secular Eden both geographically near and chronologically remote. Since so little was known about the ancient Britons, they could be plausibly offered by Garth and his fellow poets as exemplars of that happier time "Ere right and wrong, by turns, set prices bore; / And conscience had its rate like common whore" (ll. 118-19). But Garth's purpose in this section of *Claremont* is not so much to celebrate ancient virtue as to castigate modern vice, and so his tone toward Druid society, though laudatory, stops short of the reverential. As Garth presents them, the "rough, undaunted" Britons of the past are fallen creatures like ourselves; but unlike us, they had the enormous good fortune to live before the love of "luxury" (that *bête noire* of eighteenth century moralists) had assumed its corrosive latter-day intensity. Under the circumstances, Garth finds it quite natural to leaven his admiration with a certain amused condescension, as in his laconic observation that the Druid's "dress was monstrous, and fig-leaves the mode; / And quality put on no paint but woad" (ll. 90-91).

Garth goes on to explain that the Druids, like "the Samian sage" (i.e., Epicurus), held "That matter no annihilation knows"

(l. 172), and so they based their religion on the tenet "that the soul not dies, but shifts her seat, / New rounds of life to run, or past repeat" (ll. 190-91). In pursuit of that religion, they sought out holy places, among them the future site of Claremont, then a "solemn wood" of lofty oaks adorned with sacred mistletoe. Here the pious would assemble to worship and to hear their priests rehearse the stirring history (both past and yet to come) of this consecrated ground.

> Beneath the shady covert of an oak,
> In rhymes uncouth, prophetic truths they spoke.
> Attend then, Clare; nor is the legend long;
> The story of thy villa is their song.
>
> (ll. 201-4)

In his brief preface to *Claremont* Garth had remarked that "The situation [of the earl's new estate] is so agreeable and surprizing, that it inclines one to think some place of this nature put Ovid at first upon the story of Narcissus and Echo."[8] Similarly inspired and taking his cue from Ovid's tale, Garth offers a sequel, the story of Montano and Echo, which is designed to fulfill his earlier promise to explain how "Claremont" came by its name. In predicating an Ovidian derivation for an English place name, Garth had ample precedent among his fellow topographical poets; a celebrated passage in Pope's *Windsor Forest*, for example, tells of how the nymph Lodona, in order to escape being ravished by Pan, dissolved herself into a river (the Lodden) which has since borne her name. Needless to say, improbable etymologies of this sort were offered not as factual truths, but as poetic allegories whose validity lay in their beauty and aptness rather than in their plausibility.

Garth's tale (comprising the fourth section of his poem) takes us back to that distant age (ancient even to the Druids) when the Surrey hills and forests were populated by nymphs, dryads, and other such creatures from classical mythology. In the precincts of what will one day be Claremont there lives the "fair Montano, of the sylvan race" (l. 205), the offspring of a faun and a naiad. Because of his physical beauty ("Not lovlier seem'd Narcissus to the eye"—l. 211), Montano is pursued by all the woodland nymphs, though he ignores their love and devotes all his time to hunting. One day, as he ranges the forest, he comes upon a grotto "with hoary moss o'ergrown, / Rough with rude shells, and arch'd with mouldering stone" (ll. 235-36). Here he finds Echo, who has retired to this melancholy place to brood over her rejection by Narcissus. At sight of the pensive nymph, Montano is smitten by love's "keenest dart"; but when he declares himself to Echo, she abruptly flees. Thus spurned, the heartbroken Montano grows ever more disconsolate and eventually expires, but not before he has called upon his "kindred deities" to punish the "tyrant virgin" for her cruelty. To mark Montano's grave, Faunus builds a noble hill, and each of the "rural powers" contributes a suitable embellishment—Pales covers the "wond'rous pile" with luxuriant greenery; Flora strews the summit with flowers; a naiad provides a stream; and nymphs, transformed to trees, add their shade. Lastly Echo, who by now "laments her rigour" (l. 285), comes back and "haunts the lonely dales" (l. 294) in mourning for Montano. In time, she fades away until only her voice remains eternally grieving in the rocks.

The exact connection between these events and the name "Claremont" is not spelled out in the poem, for Garth knew he could depend upon his classically educated readers to get the point. The term "clare" derives from the Latin *clarus,* which among other things means "famous" or "celebrated." Like the English word "clear" (of which "clare" is an archaic form), *clarus* bears an additional sense of "unsullied" or "immaculate." The "mont" in "Claremont" refers both to Montano (cf., the Latin *montanus*—"of the mountain") and to his grave site, the hill upon which the earl of Clare's mansion is built. Thus, Garth invites his readers to rise above a prosaically literal interpretation of the estate's name (i.e., "Clare's Hill"); instead we are to recognize in "Claremont" a title symbolically appropriate to a location that has been purified and made legendary by its associations.

Aside from its explanatory function, the story of Montano is a stylized performance in which Garth more or less retells Ovid's tale of Narcissus and Echo, albeit with some rearrangement of incident and personnel. Far from playing down his reliance on Ovid, Garth deliberately stresses it, both by explicit reference in his preface (quoted above) and by reincarnating Echo (who, in Ovid's account, had perished after being rejected by Narcissus) to serve as his heroine. Yet if Garth's story of love-stricken nymphs and fauns is openly patterned on Ovid, the two are not altogether alike in tone; for Garth's unsentimental temperament produces a degree of detachment toward his material. Doubtless

Garth hopes we will find his story touching, as well as apt, but he is also fully aware that there is something comic in these woodland lovers with their alternatingly glacial and volcanic emotions. Since Garth is not writing a burlesque, he does not choose to exploit that comedy in any obvious way, but he cannot resist an occasional ironic aside. Thus we learn that the vehemence of Montano's love for Echo is in direct proportion to her initial indifference, which leads Garth to deliver some homey advice (ll. 225-34) on the romantic advantages of playing hard to get. And when at the climax of the story Echo fades away, Garth wryly notes that "Her sex's privilege she yet retains; / And, though to nothing wasted, voice remains" (ll. 295-96).

Having explored Claremont's past, the Druids (inspired by the "Delphic god") go on to prophesy its glorious future. In this, the fifth and concluding section of the poem, we are told that "Ere twice ten centuries shall fleet away, / A Brunswick prince shall Britain's sceptre sway" (ll. 299-300). Under his benign rule, liberty, religion, and justice will flourish. Faithfully serving this gracious monarch will be that very earl of Clare who will one day build his home upon this storied ground. And, as the final lines explain:

> Oft will his leisure this retirement chuse,
> Still finding future subjects for the Muse;
> And, to record the sylvan's fatal flame,
> The place shall live in song, and Claremont be the name.
> (ll. 326-29)

In offering a panegyric to the reigning king, Garth is subscribing to a convention all but universal in the "place" poem (as in so many other Augustan genres). Analogies can be found in all of Garth's acknowledged models, both ancient and modern. As Garth points out in his 1717 introduction to Ovid: "The compliments to Augustus are very frequent in the last book . . . : as those to the same emperor are in the Georgics of Virgil, which also strike the imagination by their agreeable flattery."[9] Likewise, both Denham in *Cooper's Hill* and Pope in *Windsor Forest* had paid generous homage to their respective monarchs—namely, Charles I and Queen Anne. Aside from the demands of poetic tradition, Garth also had good reason to wish to celebrate a ruler whose politics he admired and to whose patronage he owed his recently conferred knighthood. Under the circumstances, the only surprising thing about Garth's tribute to the king are its brevity (fourteen lines) and its relative sobriety—at least as measured against the effusions Garth addresses to William III in *The Dispensary* and elsewhere. Garth's restraint, we may assume, stems not from any lack of enthusiasm for the king, but rather from an understandable desire to avoid the kind of unseemly hyperbole he had so forcefully denounced in the opening lines of his poem.

On its initial appearance Garth's *Claremont* seems to have been well-received and quickly recognized as one of the more accomplished examples of its genre in English. By 1732, when the anonymous author of *Studley Royal: The Seat of John Aislabie, Esq.* listed the most distinguished "place" poems in the language, Garth's position in the roster was secure:

> Shall *Waller's* verse St. *James's* groves refine,
> And *Windsor's Pope*, out-charm *themselves* in thine?
> Shall *Denham's* muse bloom *Cooper's* hill with bays,
> And *Claremont* shine in *Garth's* immortal Lays?[10]

In our own day, after so many changes in poetic fashion, *Claremont* has attracted little notice beyond acknowledgment of its historic importance—though at least one modern critic has called it Garth's "best poem."[11] Perhaps the warmest assessment of *Claremont* was that issued thirty-four years after Garth's death by Robert Shiells, who wrote:

The poem will survive the noble structure it celebrates, and will remain a perpetual monument of its author's learning, taste and great capacity as a poet; since, in that short work, there are innumerable beauties, and a vast variety of sentiments easily and happily interwoven; the most lively strokes of satire being intermixed with the most courtly panegyric, at the same time that there appears the true spirit of enthusiasm, which distinguishes the works of one born a poet, from those of a witty, or learned man that has arrived at no higher art than that of making verse.[12]

Not all twentieth-century readers will wish to second Shiells's unqualified endorsement, but his prophetic accuracy, at any rate, is not to be denied: for *Claremont* has quite literally managed to "survive the noble structure it celebrates." When the duke of Newcastle died in 1768, the title became extinct, and the estate was sold to Lord Clive, who thereupon razed Vanbrugh's building to make room for the new edifice that occupies the site today.

II *The Occasional Verse*[13]

In 1712 the author of *The Story of the St. Alban's Ghost* undertook a mock defense of Garth against those who lamented the alleged qualitative decline in his post-*Dispensary* verse. ". . . it is very probable," we are told, that "those refined pieces that the doctor has been pleased to own, since the writing of the Dispensary, have been looked upon by the lewd debauched critics of the town to be dull and insipid, for no other reason but because they are grave and sober."[14] The gravity and sobriety here sarcastically ascribed to Garth's occasional verse are, in fact, largely limited to a handful of political poems whose Whiggish sentiments seem to have offended the Tory author of *St. Alban's Ghost.* The majority of Garth's shorter verse, as we shall see, is anything but ponderous; and if no great claims can be made for these works as literature, they remain frequently amusing and usually instructive for the light they cast on Garth's character and opinions.

"To the Merry Poetaster" (1700) is Garth's contribution to a literary battle which had in part been precipitated by *The Dispensary* (see chapter 1). It will be recalled that in canto 4 Garth's fellow physician, Sir Richard Blackmore, was pilloried as "the Bard." Blackmore responded with *A Satyr Against Wit* (1699), wherein Garth and all such "frivolous," "impious," and "indecent" writers were denounced. The reply to Blackmore's broadside attack came in the form of a volume of mock *Commendatory Verses* in which the poets Blackmore had disparaged took turns paying ironic homage to his "sober solid Principles, and . . . twenty thousand Verses . . . without one Grain of Wit in them."[15] In this collection (which he probably helped supervise) appeared Garth's "To the Merry Poetaster at Sadlers-Hall in Cheapside." The latter phrase refers to Blackmore's unfashionable home address, which had earned him the nickname, "the Cheapside Knight." In his brief and witty poem, Garth, after hailing Blackmore as one whose "censures praise" and whose "flatteries abuse" (l. 2), helpfully advises his colleague to "scribble not again" (l. 5), and thus to spare himself the painful realization that his poems, like his patients, are doomed to quick extinction. It would seem that of all Garth's insults, this slur against his medical skills piqued Blackmore most; for when he prepared a volume of *Discommendatory Verses, on Those Which are Truly Commendatory* (1700), he retaliated in verses addressed "To the Sorry Poetaster at *Will's* Coffee-House," in which Garth is described as a "Quack" whose murderous incompetence is rendered harmless only by his inability to attract any patients.[16]

Among the more charming of Garth's occasional poems are those he wrote to be inscribed upon toasting glasses for the Kit-Cat Club. It had become a custom at the Kit-Cat dinners to offer ceremonial toasts in honor of women (most often members' relatives) whose beauty or grace seemed to call for special commemoration. Each lady so complimented was assigned an individual glass on which were engraved her name and the necessarily brief verses composed in her honor by one or another member. As John Charlton described it to Lady Granby in a letter of November 4, 1703: ". . . now I am on the Kitcat, 'tis proper to tell your Ladyship that a great number of glasses are chose and a set number of ladys names are writ on them, and as an addition some fine thing is to be said on every lady, and writ there to."[17] Most such verses proved to be as perishable as the glasses they were written on, but some fifty-four have been preserved in Tonson's *Miscellany Poems* (1716) under the collective title "Verses Written for the Toasting-Glasses of the Kit-kat Club, in the Year 1703." Of these, seven (ranging from four to six lines) are by Garth: two each to the Ladies Anne Carlisle, Mary Essex, and Jane Hyde, and one to Lady Anne Wharton. In suitably generous terms, Garth professes to find the beauty of these ladies more intoxicating than the wine used to celebrate it. Characteristic is his toast to Lady Wharton:

> When Jove to Ida did the gods invite,
> And in immortal toasting pass'd the night,

> With more than nectar he the banquet bless'd,
> For Wharton was the Venus of the feast.
>
> (ll. 1-4)

Doubtless Norman Moore is correct in dismissing Garth's Kit-Cat toasts as "intended to be read only by men far advanced in postprandial potations,"[18]—though a more indulgent critic might feel that to pass so admonitory a judgment on such fragile productions was to break a butterfly upon the wheel.

Somewhat more elaborate than the Kit-Cat toasts, but in a similar spirit, are two other poems addressed by Garth to women: "To the Duchess of Bolton, On Her Staying All the Winter in the Country" and "To the Lady Louisa Lenos: With Ovid's Epistles." In the first of these, Henrietta (third wife of Charles, duke of Bolton) is urged to return as soon as possible to London, where British heroes, recently so indomitable in battle, will perforce be vanquished by her beauty: "The brave must to the fair now yield the prize, / And English arms submit to English eyes" (ll. 12-13). The "Lady Louisa Lenos" of the second poem is Louisa Lennox, the daughter of Charles, duke of Richmond. Since Garth refers to Lady Louisa's "unpractis'd years" (l. 23) and to the time "ere long" (l. 29) when her beauty will come to full flower, the poem was presumably written when its recipient (b. 1694) was still an adolescent. In the forty-one line poem Garth, assuming the manner of Matthew Prior, wittily recommends Ovid as a guide to the differing approaches men and women take toward love: "Impartial Nature equally decrees: / You have your pride, and we our perjuries" (ll. 19-20).

Garth's forty-two line "To Richard Earl of Burlington, With Ovid's Art of Love" might well be considered as a companion piece to the verses for "Lady Lenos." Again we find Garth offering Ovid to a young aristocrat as an introductory text on love (though since the pupil in this case is a male, Garth finds the clinical *Art of Love* more suitable than the romantic *Epistles*). Like Lady Louisa, Burlington (who was born in 1695 and who acceded to his title when he was nine) is addressed as one on the verge of adulthood. In his advice to Burlington, Garth's emphasis is on the pitfalls of love: "Though you possess all Nature's gifts, take care, / Love's queen has charms, but fatal is her snare" (ll. 19-20). Comparing love to the sea—whose false smiles often lure travelers to stormy destruction—Garth counsels his young friend not to let passion dictate the choice "When coming time shall bless you with a bride" (l. 31). Instead, Burlington should take his cue from Ovid's work, which illustrates the abiding truth: "She has most charms who is the most sincere" (l. 34).

Of a more public nature than the foregoing are the four poems Garth designed to be spoken from the stage as prologues or epilogues to plays. The earliest of these, the "Prologue to [Nicholas Rowe's] *Tamerlane*," was written in 1701. Rowe's tragedy was produced in December of that year and first printed in January, 1702; but on neither occasion was Garth's prologue used. Though the play was in part meant allegorically (with the heroic Tamerlane representing William III), Garth's prologue was evidently considered more overtly partisan than seemed judicious, and so it was replaced by Rowe's own more discreet effort. Garth's prologue, written just as the War of the Spanish Succession was getting underway, is an emotional call for Englishmen to rally behind William in the fight against Louis XIV. Those at home who have opposed William, Garth denounces not only as ingrates, but as near traitors: "Britons, for shame! your factious feuds decline. / Too long you've labour'd for the Bourbon line" (ll. 19-20). Since the war offers a chance for England's "lost honour" (l. 25) to be retrieved, Garth calls upon his countrymen to "Quit your cabals . . . , and in spight / Of Whig and Tory in this cause unite" (ll. 27-28).

Very different in tone is Garth's second theatrical piece, the "Prologue to *Squire Trelooby*" (1704). The play was an adaptation by Vanbrugh, Congreve, and Walsh of Molière's *Monsieur de Pourceagnac* (1699).[19] Written only a few years after Jeremy Collier's *A Short View of the Immorality and Profaneness of the English Stage* (1698), Garth's prologue defends the theater by ridiculing its would-be rehabilitators.

> There the dread phalanx of reformers come,
> Sworn foes to wit, as Carthage was to Rome;
> Their ears so sanctify'd, no scenes can please,
> But heavy hymns, or pensive homilies.
>
> (ll. 3-6)

Garth exhorts playwrights to withstand the onslaught, and he contemptuously describes "those precise Tartuffs" (l. 27) who complain of immorality on the stage as more interested in money

The Other Works

than morals: "Gold only can their pious spite allay, / They call none criminals that can but pay" (ll. 30-31).

The occasion of Garth's third prologue was not a new play, but rather a new playhouse. To Garth and his fellow Kit-Cats (many of whom were either playwrights or patrons of the drama), the opening of the Haymarket Theatre on April 9, 1705, was an event of special satisfaction.[20] Club members (including Garth) had been the major subscribers toward the building of the playhouse, and Vanbrugh was to be its first manager. At the theater's inaugural performance—the play was James Shirley's *The Gamester*—Garth's "Prologue Spoken at the Opening of the Queen's Theatre in the Haymarket" was recited by the celebrated actress, Anne Bracegirdle. In the first lines of his poem Garth congratulates the architect of the theater, but goes on to point out that only poets "can duration give: / When marble falls, the Muses' structures live" (ll. 5-6). Obliquely, but unmistakably, Garth renews his attack on Collier and his fellow reformers (most of them clergymen):

> In the good age of ghostly ignorance,
> How did cathedrals rise, and zeal advance!
> . . . .
> Pardons for sins were purchas'd with estates,
> And none but rogues in rags dy'd reprobates.
> (ll. 13-14, 17-18)

Happily, such "pious pageantry's no more" (l. 19), having been replaced by the innocent pageantry of the theater—such as the "Majestic columns" (l. 22), the "carrs triumphal" (l. 23), the "Descending goddesses" (l. 26), and the "gilt machines" (l. 27) that Garth predicts will in time be seen on the Haymarket stage. The anticlerical tenor of Garth's remarks so offended the Tory journalist Charles Leslie that in *The Rehearsal*, No. 41 he denounced the prologue, explaining that it was "said to be Written by Dr. *G[ar]th*, Chaplain to *Kit-Kat*, an Open and Profess'd Enemy to all Religion."[21]

The last of Garth's theater pieces was his "Epilogue to the Tragedy of *Cato*" (1713). Since *Cato*'s author, Joseph Addison, was a prominent Whig, the play's first performance was before an audience that expected to see a highly political drama full of precise contemporary applications. In fact, *Cato* (most of which

Addison had written ten years earlier) was relatively free of allegorical intent; however, partisan Whigs and Tories were quick to read current meanings into the text and to issue their applause accordingly. Luckily for Addison, each faction interpreted the play to its own advantage. Thus Cato, the heroic champion of liberty, struck the Whigs as the very embodiment of Marlborough; while the Tories professed to find in him a strong resemblance to the earl of Oxford. After the opening performance, both Whigs and Tories gave money to Barton Booth, the actor who played Cato: "So betwixt them," Pope wrote to John Caryll on April 30, 1713, " 'tis probable that Cato (as Dr. Garth expressed it) may have something to live upon, after he dies."[22]

In contrast to the somber dignity of the play to which it is attached, Garth's epilogue strikes a light satiric note. Spoken by Mary Porter, the epilogue ruefully condemns the "odd fantastic things we women do" (l. 1) in matters of love. Too often, it seems, women allow wealth to take precedence over natural affections, with the result that "He sighs with most success that settles well" (l. 16). Men, however, are equally money-minded: "Your breasts no more the fire of beauty warms, / But wicked wealth usurps the power of charms" (ll. 21-22). In closing, both sexes are urged to restore the standards of that happier age "When words were artless, and the thoughts sincere" (l. 31).

More than a century after Garth wrote his epilogue, Macaulay described it as "ignoble and out of place"[23] in conjunction to so serious a drama as *Cato*—a judgment that seems both unduly harsh and ahistorical. For as a modern critic of the eighteenth-century English theater points out: "it early became the practice that tragedy should be introduced by a stately prologue and that the epilogue should remain frivolous."[24] Such was certainly the case with *Cato*, which was introduced by a suitably dignified prologue written by Pope. In *The Guardian*, No. 33 Steele (after commending Pope for the nobility of his prologue) found it equally appropriate to praise how "Dr. Garth has very agreeably rallied the mercenary traffic between men and women of this age in the epilogue."[25]

Considering the degree of Garth's political involvement, it is somewhat surprising to find that only a few of his occasional poems are on specifically political subjects. Four poems fall into this category: "On the King of Spain," "To the Earl of

Godolphin," "On Her Majesty's Statue," and "On the New Conspiracy."[26] Of these, the poem "On the King of Spain" (1706) is first chronologically, though at six lines it is little more than a casual epigram. In it Garth commemorates the lifting of the siege of Barcelona, where English troops had come to the relief of the Archduke Charles, Hapsburg claimant to the Spanish throne and the future Emperor Carlos VI. His countrymen's heroic efforts on behalf of an erstwhile enemy nation inspire Garth to compare the English to Pallas Athena, who acted both as scourge and savior to the Trojans: "Thus the fam'd empire where the Iber flows, / Fell by Eliza, and by Anna rose" (ll. 5-6).

Of a more substantial nature is the set of verses Garth wrote to console the earl of Godolphin on his removal as lord treasurer. Garth, who esteemed Godolphin as a Whig and a fellow Kit-Cat, was distressed when on August 8, 1710, Queen Anne abruptly dismissed the earl from the office he had held for eight years. In commemorating this event Garth could hardly afford to be so impolitic as to criticize the queen's action directly, and so he devotes the first twenty lines of his thirty-two line poem to extolling Godolphin and his conduct in office: "Our isle enjoys, by your successful care, / The pomp of peace, amidst the woes of war" (ll. 3-4). In the latter part of the poem, however, Garth speaks darkly of how "some star, sinister to our prayers, / Contrives new schemes and calls you from affairs" (ll. 21-22). In closing, Garth sadly notes that though "Ingratitude's a weed of every clime" (l. 27), in time Godolphin will be vindicated.

So disturbing did the Tories find Garth's poem that Matthew Prior devoted most of *The Examiner*, No. 6 (September 7, 1710) to an attack upon this "curious Piece of Poetical Workmanship."[27] Though Prior affects a fastidious distaste for Garth's grammar, diction, and imagery, it is the poem's implied criticism of the queen that draws the sharpest rebuke. After quoting Garth's line on the universality of ingratitude, Prior indignantly writes: "But who is to be charg'd with this Ingratitude? The whole Body of the Nation did indeed wish the T[reasure]r out; but 'twas Her Majesty only that could displace him. Such are the Complements [*sic*] which the Crown receives from this *Antimonarchical* Academy. Excellent Poets, dutiful Subjects."[28]

Prior's attack was not answered by Garth, but by Addison, who in *The Whig Examiner*, No. 1 (September 14, 1710) excoriates *The Examiner* for the "cavilling spirit" of its criticism: "We are now in an age wherein impudent assertions must pass for arguments: and I do not question, but the same who has endeavoured here to prove, that he who wrote the Dispensary was no poet, will very suddenly undertake to shew, that he who gained the battle of Blenheim is no general."[29] Predictably, Prior answered with an attack on Addison, which in turn inspired a counterattack. In this exchange, Garth and his poem to Godolphin were soon left behind, but not until Prior's sneers had elicited from Addison a fervent endorsement of Garth's poetic talents. In answer to Prior's contention that Addison and his "brother" Garth were equally incompetent as poets, Addison grandly replied (*The Tatler*, No. 239, October 19, 1710): "I think myself as much honoured by being joined . . . with the gentleman whom he here calls my brother, as I am in the beginning [of Prior's attack], by being mentioned with Horace and Virgil."[30] Dr. Johnson, taking a more detached view, concludes that Garth's "To the Earl of Godolphin" deserves preservation more "for the sake of [Addison's] vindication"[31] than for its own artistic merits.

The resentment against Queen Anne which could only be hinted at in the verses to Godolphin finds much fuller expression in "On Her Majesty's Statue in St. Paul's Church-Yard" (1715). Like most Whigs, Garth had felt betrayed when the queen shifted her allegiance to the Tories. Her dismissal of Godolphin was followed by the even more "ungrateful" removal of Marlborough as general of the army. To the dismay of the Whigs, she lent her support to the Tory Peace of Utrecht—a settlement whose concessions to the French many Whigs considered treasonously excessive. By 1715, with Anne dead and his party back in power, Garth no longer felt obliged to disguise his scorn, and when a memorial statue of the queen was erected at the north end of St. Paul's, he responded with what is perhaps the best of his occasional poems. In "On Her Majesty's Statue" there is nothing of the good-natured bantering tone so frequent in Garth's satire: instead, the poem conveys a mordant and icy disdain. Garth opens by describing the statue, at whose feet are symbolic representations of several nations. Each nation looks up in homage to the queen, with one exception; for "France alone with downcast eyes is seen" (l. 9). The bulk of the poem is addressed to France in reproof for her unseemly stance:

The Other Works

> Ungrateful country! to forget so soon,
> All that great Anna for thy sake has done:
> When sworn the kind defender of thy cause,
> Spite of her dear religion, spite of laws;
> For thee she sheath'd the terrours of her sword,
> For thee she broke her general—and her word:
> For thee her mind in doubtful terms she told,
> And learn'd to speak like oracles of old.
> For thee, for thee alone, what could she more?
> She lost the honour she had gain'd before.
>
> (ll. 11-20)

The poem closes with the statement: "For thee in annals she's content to shine,/Like other monarchs of the Stuart line" (ll. 25-26)—a couplet whose "crushing mildness," in the opinion of one recent critic, made it "a fit harbinger of the Hanoverians."[32]

A less controlled (and hence less effective) poem is the last of Garth's political verses, "On the New Conspiracy, 1716," addressed to his "degenerate countrymen" (l. 1) who had joined in the Jacobite rebellion of the previous year. The emotional tenor of the poem may be gauged by the angry sarcasm Garth applies to those who preferred the Pretender to George I: "O! noble passion, to your country kind,/To crown her with—the refuse of mankind" (ll. 9-10). The rebels are grimly warned that if they continue to "tempt the great avenger's blow" (l. 15) and "Madly . . . try to weaken George's reign" (l. 27), they will be crushed; for "By right, by worth, by wonders, made our own,/The hand that gave it shall preserve his throne" (ll. 29-30).

In addition to the occasional poems already mentioned, four other brief pieces by Garth have survived. The "Prologue to the Music-Meeting in the York Buildings" commemorates a concert by two unidentified female singers: "Here their soft magic those two Syrens try,/And if we listen, or but look, we die" (ll. 3-4). In "A Soliloquy Out of Italian" a love-stricken young lady bemoans the social convention that prevents her from admitting to her suitor "how fondly I return his flame" (l. 3). "An Imitation of a French Author" proclaims that Marlborough's heroic acts are as numerous as a "bridegroom's joys or miser's cares,/Or gamester's oaths, or hermit's prayers" (ll. 7-8). And finally, in an "Anacreontic Epistle to Mr. Gay" (ca. 1717) that poet is praised as one who has "transcrib'd what Phoebus sung" (l. 8)—thus

Garth returns almost the same compliment he had himself received in "To Bernard Lintot" (1712), where Gay had written: "Great *Phoebus* in his learned Son [i.e., Garth] we see."[33]

As should be apparent from the above survey, Garth's occasional poems are not without their merits. The same ironic wit and talent for epigram that Garth had displayed in *The Dispensary* enliven many of these brief works as well, and in at least one poem—"On Her Majesty's Statue"—Garth achieves a satiric intensity not often found elsewhere in his work. Yet it would be an exaggeration to suggest that these slight pieces, either individually or collectively, contribute very much to Garth's stature as a poet. For all their frequent charm and considerable poetic skill, it is primarily as reflections of Garth's opinions, interests, and tastes that these by-products of a busy career deserve our attention.

III "Roman Eloquence": Garth as a Translator

To the body of Garth's works already discussed must be added his two excursions into Latin composition and his three English renditions of Greek and Latin originals. His very debut as an author was with the *Oratio Laudatoria in Aedibus Collegii Regalis Med. Lond.* (1697); and in the opening years of the new century he published translations of Plutarch's "Life of Otho" (1700) and Demosthenes' "First Philippick" (1702). Almost a decade later, as part of a proposed new edition of Lucretius, Garth composed a Latin dedication addressed to the future George I. The last and by far the most ambitious of Garth's classical forays was a new English version of the *Metamorphoses* (1717), for which Garth served as general editor and translator of 902 of Ovid's 12,000 lines.[34]

Like any classically educated gentleman of his time, Garth had received a solid grounding in Latin and at least a usable knowledge of Greek. The evidence of his translations and original compositions suggests that in Latin, at any rate, Garth could claim something more than mere competence—though not all his contemporaries were willing to concede as much. It will be remembered that Garth's Latin eulogy for Dryden (which the *Post-Boy* of May 14, 1700, thought "eloquent") was dismissed by Edward Hinton for its "false Latin"[35] and by Thomas Hearne for its "many Blunders in the Pronunciation."[36] Beside these jaundiced assessments of Garth's Latin skills, however, we may place the opinion of John Bell, who in 1779 wrote that the "sentiments, the spirit, and style" of Garth's Harveian Oration demonstrated his "perfect acquaintance with antiquity, and correct taste in Roman eloquence."[37] While relatively few readers or critics today are qualified to judge such matters personally, an examination of Garth's translations suggests that neither the sneers nor the compliments are altogether justified; for if Garth's classical exercises seldom achieve brilliance, they do not often fall below proficiency.

In the *Oratio Laudatoria* (delivered on September 17, 1697, and published shortly thereafter)[38] Garth conscientiously observes the terms under which William Harvey had in 1656 endowed an annual Latin lecture to be presented before the assembled College of Physicians. That lecture, Harvey specified, should fulfill three main functions: (1) "a commemoration of . . . the benefactors of the said College," (2) a call for the members "to search and study out the secrets of nature," and (3) an expostulation to those in the profession "to continue in mutual love and affection among themselves."[39] In keeping with these instructions Garth devotes his brief address—less than 3,000 words—to (1) a formal eulogy to King William, (2) an injunction to physicians to rescue the art of healing from medical quacks, and (3) a call to the disaffected "Apothecaries Physicians" to rejoin the majority of the college in support of the dispensary project.

Although Garth opens his *Oratio* with a modest reference to himself as one "qui neque doctrina neque arte dicendi polleam,"[40] it is apparent that he conscientiously strove to make his discourse not merely correct, but graceful. The manuscript of his final English draft before translation has survived,[41] and its numerous deletions, substitutions, and emendations reflect the author's concern for smoothness of sound and cadence. A stylistic device Garth puts to recurrent use is the carefully balanced series of clauses, most often in sets of three. Thus, in a representative example, he phrases his denunciation of medical mountebanks as follows (in the English draft): "But this Troop of Cheats wounds not with Weapons, but with a certain more destructive Theriac [i.e., derived from animals] Medicine; they contend not by Fire—but some forreign powders, they kill not with Bullets, but with Pills as fatal."[42] This, in the Latin text, becomes: "Non autem telis vulnerat ista Agyrtarum colluvies, sed Theriaca quadam magis perniciosa, non pyrio, sed pulvere nescio quo exotico certat, non globulis plumbeis, sed pilulis aeque lethalibus interficit."[43] The paragraph in which these lines occur seemed so impressive to the editors of the *Biographica Britannica* (1747-1766) that they reprinted it in full, along with what Samuel Johnson felt was "more praise than the passage . . . will fully justify." Johnson's own lack of enthusiasm for Garth's Latin prose style is apparent in his remark (after quoting the lines cited above) that "This was certainly thought fine by the author, and is still admired by his biographer."[44]

Garth's earliest published translations of classical originals were from Greek, rather than Latin works. Between 1683 and 1686 there had appeared a five-volume edition of *Plutarch's Lives, Translated From the Greek by Several Hands*—sometimes referred to as the "Dryden" Plutarch after its most famous contributor. Garth had no role in this translation until 1700: at that time the work was reissued in a third edition which included (with other revisions) Garth's new translation of the "Life of Otho," replacing the Thomas Beaumont version used earlier. Likewise, in 1702 Garth contributed the "First Philippick" to *Several Orations of Demosthenes, To Encourage the Athenians to Oppose the Exorbitant Power of Philip of Macedon, English'd from the Greek by Several Hands*. As English renditions of the works in question, Garth's translations from the Greek seem (at least to the nonexpert) to be stiffly competent, rather than distinguished; for they have about them the faintly laborious air of conscientiously performed schoolboy assignments. Moreover, in the case of the "First Philippick," the impulse behind the translation was at least as much political as literary. As its full title suggests, Demosthenes' *Several Orations* (issued just as England was reembarking on a war with France) was intended by its Whig sponsors to help in rallying the nation against that latter-day Philip of Macedon, Louis XIV.

In 1711 Garth issued a Latin prose *Epitaphium Lucretii Editionis*, dedicating a proposed new edition of that author's *De Rerum Natura* to the "Serenissimo Principi, Georgio Ludovico Bruns. & Lun. Duci, &c."[45] It is not clear whether Garth's role in this planned edition went beyond writing the dedication, though there is ambiguous evidence suggesting that Garth himself was the intended editor. In 1713 *La Histoire Critique de la*

République des Lettres describes the work as in progress under Garth's direction: "*Mr. G fameux Docteur en Medecine travaille a nous donner une nouvelle edition de Lucrèce.*"[46] If this account (for which there is no confirmation) is true, Garth must have soon thereafter abandoned the project; for the proposed edition never materialized. Ironically, however, the nonexistent "Garth" edition of Lucretius has found its way into a number of bibliographies, wherein Garth is mistakenly credited with having produced the 1712 quarto edition of Lucretius published by Tonson. Thus, *A Bibliographical Dictionary* (Manchester, 1803) not only lists a 1712 Lucretius "ex edit. Sam. Garthii," but commends the editor for his book's handsome format and illustrations.[47]

In the *Epitaphium* itself Garth addresses the future George I in the florid terms suitable to such literary occasions, employing a Latin style notably more ornate than that he had used for the declamatory *Oratio Laudatoria*. In a characteristic passage, Garth modestly explains: "Quamplurimi forsan putent, dignitatis tuae me parum rationem habere, qui, quicquid forte deliraverim, augusto tuo nomini consecrare voluerim; sed & clementiam tuam & tenuitatem meam juxta novi."[48] The *Epitaphium* seems to have been well-received, particularly by those who supported the Hanoverian succession. In 1714, when George assumed the throne, the work was reissued (along with an English translation by John Oldmixon), and as late as 1753 we find Robert Shiells referring to Garth's *Epitaphium* as "one of the purest compositions in the Latin tongue that our times have produced."[49]

In his earlier translations from Plutarch and Demosthenes, Garth's role had been that of a minor participant in collective efforts directed by others: however, for the imposing new English verse rendition of Ovid's *Metamorphoses* published in 1717, Garth not only translated a substantial 902 lines, but also served as general editor—in which capacity he wrote the critical essay that introduces the work. The idea for a new edition of the *Metamorphoses* seems to have originated with Tonson, who over the years had informally assembled a number of partial translations (independently done by Dryden, Addison, and others) comprising roughly half of Ovid's 12,000 lines. About 1714, presumably at Tonson's behest, Garth undertook to help solicit the remaining translations and to lend his name and efforts to the project as general editor. The only surviving record of negotiations between Garth or Tonson with the translators consists of two 1715 letters in which we find first Tonson and then Garth enlisting the services of James Vernon to translate the latter portions of book 8.[50] An amusing glimpse of Garth's efforts to recruit translators is found in Pope's "Sandys's Ghost: Or a Proper New Ballad on the New Ovid's Metamorphosis [sic]" (1716). In that poem, the spirit of George Sandys (who had translated Ovid in 1621-1626) describes how "*Garth* at *St. James's*, and at *White*'s / Beats up for Volunteers" to help complete his edition.[51] The satiric burden of Pope's poem is that Garth and Tonson, in their haste to get the job done, may wind up doing violence to Ovid. Pope's misgivings, however, did not prevent him from translating the brief fable of Dryope (book 9) for the new edition.

In the summer of 1717 the long-anticipated translation— dedicated to Princess Caroline and introduced by Garth's critical preface—finally appeared. In that preface, Garth proclaims himself "an advocate for Ovid, who I think is too much run down at present by the critical spirit of this nation."[52] By way of correction, Garth devotes the bulk of his preface to an appreciative survey (with extensive quotations) of Ovid's special "beauties"—his descriptive eloquence, his emotional sublety, and his moral instructiveness. Garth's advocacy, however, is less than total, and he intersperses his praise with pointed criticism of what he calls Ovid's "boyisms"—i.e., the overelaborate images and verbal extravagancies which, in Garth's opinion, blemish the *Metamorphoses*. Such faults, along with Ovid's general exuberance of invention, have produced, says Garth, the work's major flaw: its prolixity. After wishing that Ovid, "instead of saying all he could, had only said all he should,"[53] Garth concludes "that the author left [the *Metamorphoses*] unfinished; if it had undergone his last hand, it is more than probable that many superfluities had been retrenched."[54]

For his own section of the translation (book 14 and the tale of Cippus in book 15) Garth was faced with a task much more complex than that involved in his earlier prose translations; for transforming Ovid's Latin dactylic hexameters into English iambic pentameter couplets called for something more than simple literal accuracy. In his preface, after remarking that translations are "commonly either verbal, or paraphrase, or imitation," Garth explains that "The manner that seems most suited for this present undertaking, is, neither to follow the author too close out of a critical timourousness; nor abandon him too wantonly through a poetic boldness. The original should always be kept in view, without too apparent a deviation from the sense. Where it is otherwise, it is not a version, but an imitation."[55] Yet despite this espousal of the happy middleground, Garth's own translation (as we might have foreseen from his strictures on Ovid's "superfluities") shows a notable willingness to "improve" upon the Latin text.

In what is perhaps his most striking departure from the original, Garth regularly abridges Ovid's text by eliminating much of the peripheral descriptive and narrative detail. The result, in the opinion of William Dwyer, is that Garth's rendering "reads like a synopsis of the Latin."[56] The extent and nature of Garth's omissions can best be seen in a characteristic passage: early in book 14 Circe, angry that Glaucus has rejected her in favor of Scylla, reacts as is shown in Frank J. Miller's literal translation:

> . . . she straightway bruised together uncanny herbs with juices of dreadful power, singing while she mixed them Hecate's own charms. Then, donning an azure cloak, she took her way from her palace through the throng of beasts that fawned upon her as she passed, and made for Rhegium, lying opposite Zancle's rocky coast. She fared along the seething waters, on which she trod as on the solid ground, skimming dry-shod along the surface of the sea. There was a little pool, curving into a deep bow, a peaceful place where Scylla loved to come. Thither would she betake her from the heat of sea and sky, when the sun at his strongest was in mid-heaven, and from his zenith had drawn the shadows to their shortest compass. This pool, before the maiden's coming, the goddess befouls and tinctures with her baleful poisons. When these had been poured out she sprinkles liquors brewed from noxious roots, and a charm, dark with its maze of uncanny words, thrice nine times she murmurs over with lips well skilled in magic.[57]

As rendered by Garth, the same passage becomes:

> Some fascinating bev'rage now she brews;
> Compos'd of deadly drugs, and baneful juice.
> At Rhegium she arrives; the ocean braves,
> And treads with unwet feet the boiling waves.
> Upon the beach a winding bay there lies,
> Shelter'd from seas, and shaded from the skies:

> This station Scylla chose: a soft retreat
> From chilling winds, and raging Cancer's heat.
> The vengeful sorc'ress visits this recess;
> Her charms infuses, and infects the place.[58]

In such instances we see Garth drastically reducing Ovid's original by (in Dwyer's words) "systematically stripping it of all that could be called 'poetic.'"[59] Thus, while Garth's translation is not without its own expressive virtues, one inevitable effect of his synoptic approach is a sharp alteration of Ovid's tone and scale. And this effect is intensified by Garth's eighteenth-century rhetoric and diction, which tend to impose an incongruous air of formality. In the light of these facts, Dwyer finds Garth's rendition too abbreviated to pass muster as a translation and too un-Ovidian to qualify as an acceptable "imitation."[60]

As a collective effort, the Garth *Metamorphoses* is naturally uneven, and many of the criticisms made against Garth's portion are at least equally applicable to the efforts of other contributors. But if the Garth translation, from a modern perspective, seems more reflective of English than of Roman Augustanism, that very quality helped commend it to eighteenth-century readers. Despite its rivals, it was the Garth edition which became, in the words of Douglas Bush, "the chief Augustan version of the *Metamorphoses*."[61] The frequency of its reissuance (new editions in 1717, 1720, 1727, 1732, 1736, 1751, 1772, 1794, 1807, 1810, and 1818) confirms William H. Irving's description of the work as "that most popular book of the eighteenth century, Garth's *Ovid*."[62] Nor do all modern critics agree with Dwyer's contention that the translation as a whole represents a "triumph of bookselling over genuine literary impulse":[63] F. Seymour Smith calls it "the best of the eighteenth century translations of the 'Metamorphoses' . . . [with] parts which have yet to be excelled,"[64] and L. P. Wilkinson considers it "the last great monument of [Ovid's] former glory."[65] For better or worse, the Garth *Metamorphoses* must also serve as its editor's final monument; for it was his last literary effort, and within a year and a half of its publication, Sir Samuel Garth was dead.

CHAPTER 5

Garth's Influence and Reputation

I "What the General Suffrage Had Chose"

IN *The Tryal of Skill: or a New Session of the Poets* (1704), the anonymous author describes how Apollo and the Muses have assembled to determine which living poet best qualifies to occupy "Witt's Throne." Some twenty-three candidates (among them Steele, Rowe, Defoe, and Congreve) are in turn considered and rejected.

> Till *Clio* call'd out, for her *Garth* to appear,
>   Rising up with his Works in her Hand,
> And said to the God, Sh' had a Candidate there,
>   Would their Votes and their Wishes Command.
> A Bard, that for Judgment, Expression and Thought,
>   For sweetness of Style and Address,
> Had never yet known such a thing as a Fault,
>   And that only was fit for the Place.
> *Parnassus* confess'd his approach, and each Muse
>   At his Entrance transported arose,
> Nor was it in *Phoebus* to put by or refuse,
>   What the General Suffrage had chose.[1]

Nor was *The Tryal of Skill* the only contemporary session-of-the-poets work to award the crown to Garth: in *An Epistle to Sr. Richard Blackmore, Occasion'd by the Death of Mr. Dryden* (1700), Dryden's "Mantle falls to G[arth] by Destiny,"[2] and in Ned Ward's *The Secret History of Clubs* (1709), all rivals "resign the Crown when *Garth* appears."[3] Posterity (as it so often does in such matters) has taken a very different view, and in the two and one half centuries since his death, Garth's literary standing has undergone a sad, if predictable, decline.

It is a truism that critical evaluations made during an author's lifetime—especially those by his personal friends and enemies—are suspect. Certainly in Garth's case it seems obvious that the praises he received in his own day often owed something of their fervor to extraliterary considerations. Aside from his genuine merits and the enthusiasm of his friends, another factor enhancing Garth's contemporary reputation as a poet was the lucky timing of his literary debut. Within a few months of *The Dispensary*'s publication, Dryden died, thereby creating a poetic interregnum during which Garth, in the absence of any commanding rivals, seemed all the more imposing. However, with the passage of time and the gradual emergence of more formidable poets, Garth's admirers naturally became more temperate in their assessments. If we add to this the smallness of Garth's poetic production and the topicality of his major work, it should come as no surprise to find that in the years after his death Garth's literary reputation underwent a realistic adjustment downward.

There is seldom any clear consensus in such matters, but by the middle of the eighteenth century Garth's claim to a respectable position on at least the lesser slopes of Parnassus seemed secure. The continued popularity of *The Dispensary* is attested by the regularity with which new editions appeared and by the frequency with which Garth's works figured in collections and anthologies. There were those like Horace Walpole, who (in a letter of May 14, 1792) continued to rank Garth among "our very best poets";[4] while there were others like Charles Churchill, who (in *The Ghost* [1763]) dismissed him as "One GARTH who err'd in Wit and Rhime."[5] But much more common than such hyperbole were comments in which Garth was accorded the measured praise appropriate to the author of a widely acknowledged minor classic.

It would be pointless to repeat here the numerous eighteenth-century judgments of Garth and his works already quoted earlier in other contexts. A few such judgments not previously cited, however, may serve to suggest the respectful (if sometimes qualified) terms in which Garth's poetry was generally treated. Representative is William Guthrie's *The Apotheosis of Milton* (1739), a work describing a dream in which the author attended a gathering of the spirits of England's most illustrious poets. "I perceiv'd a Member who had entered unobserved by me. . . . He had a most engaging Smile, and a winning Deportment, and his Dress was composed of a very rich *French* Brocade made up in the *English* Fashion. . . . The Genius then informed me that the Person I saw was Sir *Samuel Garth*, more eminent for the productions of his Genius, than his Dignity of Knighthood."[6] Coming from an author who so obviously disapproved of Garth's politics, the compliment to his poetry takes on all the more force. To William Ayre, writing in 1745, Garth seemed "one of the Best poets of his Time";[7] and Vicesimus Knox (after complaining of "the natural monotony of French verse") remarks in 1778 that "He who reads [Voltaire's] *Henriade* and at the same time thinks of Milton, Dryden, Garth or Pope, must close the volume with all the loathing of disgust."[8] In William Hayley's *An Essay on Epic Poetry* (1782) Garth is celebrated as having redeemed the art of healing from the poetic dishonor it had suffered at the hands of Blackmore:

> Swift at the word his sprightly GARTH began
> To make an helmet of a Close-stool Pan;
> An Urinal he for his trumpet takes,
> And at each blast he blows see Laughter shakes.[9]

And at the end of the century Robert Anderson, introducing his fellow physician Garth in *The Works of the British Poets* (1793), proclaims *The Dispensary* second only to *The Rape of the Lock* "in humour, discrimination of character, and poetical ardour."[10] In one sense, even the generally deflationary tone of Johnson's "Life of Garth" may be taken as an indirect testament to Garth's continued high reputation, since it is clear that Johnson's criticisms are offered as a corrective to what he considered the extravagant praise aimed at Garth by others.

II *"Fam'd Poets" and "Unfledg'd Muses"*

Aside from direct expressions of critical opinion, a useful gauge of a poet's impact upon his age is the extent to which his example influences his fellow poets. In his verses "To Dr. Garth, on the Fourth Edition of his Incomparable Poem, *The Dispensary*" (1700), Dr. James Drake confidently predicted that Garth would exercise such influence: "Fam'd Poets after him shall strain their Throats,/And unfledg'd Muses chirp their Infant-notes."[11] Drake's prophecy was soon fulfilled; for in addition to the avowed imitations and adaptations spawned by *The Dispensary*, Garth's poem was to play an important role in developing the mock-heroic mode that came to dominate the satiric poetry of the eighteenth century.

Within a few weeks of its initial publication *The Dispensary* had inspired its first imitation, William King's *The Furmentary* (1699), and in 1701 there appeared the anonymous *The Dispensary Transvers'd*, a work in which Garth's satiric techniques and characters are reworked into an attack upon the incompetence and greed of doctors. In the same year another anonymous work took its cue from Garth: *The Dissertator in Burlesque* is a satire on contemporary politics and literature, and though the approach is more hudibrastic than mock-heroic, the author specifically acknowledges the importance of Garth's example:

> When flowing numbers, Verse Polite,
> Is labour'd to describe a fight,
> Betwixt *Apothecaries* Boys
> Engaging with *Heroic* Noise;
> Their Colours, Aprons blue display'd,
> Their Ammunition, Drugs decay'd;
> With Phyal broke, and Gally-pot,
> Instead of Gunpowder and Shot:
> Are the dire Warlike Arms they carry,
> So sung in famous *Dispensary*,
> Which in the *Canto* following Sings,
> The praises of the best of Kings.
> *Epic Burlesque*, and Satyr keen
> Dancing i' th' same Heroic mein,
> Laughter at once affords and loathing,
> Like *Shakespear's* Tincture in Lord's cloathing.[12]

Even Blackmore was willing to learn from *The Dispensary*, as is apparent in his poem *The Kit-Cats* (1708), a mock-heroic with notable echoes of Garth's phraseology and manner.

Of all the poets who were to build on Garth's example, by far the most significant was Pope. As a close friend, Pope had often expressed his affection for Garth as a man (see chapter 1); that Pope admired *The Dispensary* as well as its author can be seen by his satiric practice and his explicit acknowledgments of Garth's influence on his poetry. Pope's personal copies of the fifth (1703) and the sixth (1706) editions of *The Dispensary* have survived, and each is carefully annotated (mostly with character identifications) in Pope's hand.[13] In *The Dunciad* Pope readily concedes that he is following in Garth's poetic footsteps. In book 2 Dulness urges Edmund Curll to persist in foisting off bad poets as if they were good: "So shall each hostile name become our own, / And we too boast a Garth and Addison" (II, 131-32).[14] In his note to these lines Pope comments of himself: "It must have been particularly agreeable to him to celebrate Dr. *Garth*; both as his constant friend thro' life, and as he was his predecessor in this kind of Satire."[15] Similarly, in *A Letter to a Noble Lord* (1733) Pope remarks: "You observe, I am a mere *imitator of Homer, Horace, Boileau, Garth,* &c. (which I have the less cause to be ashamed of, since they were imitators of one another)."[16]

When Pope produced his first mock-epic, *The Rape of the Lock*, it was apparent that a close study of *The Dispensary* had taught him much about the comic possibilities of the form. We know that Pope consulted Garth while *The Rape of the Lock* was being written, for (as mentioned earlier) Pope sought and received Garth's approval for the addition of the epic machinery of sylphs and nymphs to the poem. In some measure, Pope's basic satiric stance toward the world of Arabella Fermor may even have derived from *The Dispensary*, since, as Geoffrey Tillotson points out: Pope's "theme [in *The Rape of the Lock*] entailed a fashionable setting that had been . . . memorably touched on by Garth. . . ."[17]

Even the most cursory comparison of *The Rape of the Lock* and *The Dispensary* reveals numerous points of resemblance. Not all of these, of course, need be ascribed to Garth's individual precedence, since any two writers of mock-epics, however independent, necessarily draw upon a common tradition. Yet there are many instances in which Pope can be seen quite unambiguously imitating and refining recognizable elements from Garth's poem—as, for example, in Pope's adaptation of Garth's technique of juxtaposing the serious and trivial while pretending to be oblivious to the distinction (discussed in chapter 3). To this may be added such verbal and descriptive parallels as those between *The Dispensary*'s account of the composition of matter (I, 23-52)[18] and *The Rape*'s explanation of how expired females are resolved into sylphs, nymphs, gnomes, and salamanders (I, 57-66). Likewise, the Baron's altar to Love in Pope (II, 35-46) owes much to Horoscope's altar to Disease in Garth (III, 77-86); and Umbriel's descent to the Cave of Spleen (IV, 17-54) draws a good deal from Celsus' visit to the underworld in *The Dispensary* (VI, 31-225). Beyond such examples (which could be multiplied) a sizable number of Pope's individual lines closely echo the thought and language used by Garth in *The Dispensary*. Thus, in Garth's mock battle we learn of Blackmore that: "Stunn'd with the Blow the batter'd Bard retir'd,/Sunk down, and in a Simile expir'd" (*T.N.*, 746)—while in Pope's analogue "A *Beau* and *Witling* perish'd in the Throng,/One dy'd in *Metaphor*, and one in *Song*" (V, 59-60). In the same manner, Garth's ghostly society belle who used to "Blaze in the Box, and sparkle in the Ring" (VI, 209) is an obvious prototype for Pope's erstwhile beauties (now turned into sylphs) who "Hang o'er the *Box*, and hover round the *Ring*" (I, 44).[19]

For his second great mock-epic, *The Dunciad*, Pope also drew upon *The Dispensary*, whose example he acknowledged in the statement quoted above. Ian Jack refers in passing to "the close atmosphere of *The Dispensary* (which has a good deal in common with that of the *Dunciad*) . . ."[20]—an allusion to the strong resemblances of tone and detail between the squalid lower reaches of the eighteenth-century medical and literary worlds as pictured by Garth and Pope. In *The Dispensary* (and to a lesser extent in Dryden's *MacFlecknoe*) Pope found an instructive precedent in the effective use of scatology in a mock-heroic context—a precedent that served him well in such incidents as the heroic games of book 2 of *The Dunciad*. Illustrating Pope's adaptations of Garth's scatological satire is the following example. In *The Dispensary*, when Horoscope faints, his servant empties a urinal over him:

> Whose Steam the Wight no sooner did receive,
> But rous'd, and bless'd the Stale Restorative.
> The Springs of Life their former Vigour feel,
> Such Zeal he had for that vile Utensil.
> (II, 207-10)

In *The Dunciad* Edmund Curll draws equivalent strength from the sewage of Fleet Ditch:

> Renew'd by ordure's sympathetic force,
> As oil'd with magic juices for the course,

> Vig'rous he rises; from th'effluvia strong
> Imbibes new life, and scours and stinks along.
>
> (II, 95-98)

And in addition to such parallels, *The Dunciad* has its share of close verbal echoes of individual lines from *The Dispensary*—e.g., Garth's "How ductile Matter new Meanders takes" (I, 25) and Pope's "And ductile dulness new meanders takes" (I, 62); or Garth's "With Godhead born, but curs'd, that cannot die!" (I, 106) and Pope's "For born a Goddess, Dulness never dies" (I, 16).[21]

Tracing Garth's specific influence on poets after Pope is often an exercise in the problematic, since it is easy to be misled into assigning Garthian origins to works which more probably reflect Garth's example only insofar as it was transmuted and improved upon by Pope. There are, however, a number of works of the middle and late eighteenth century that show Garth, in spite of Pope's overshadowing, still attracting his own imitators—as, for example, in *The Prophetic Physician: An Heroi-Comic Poem Address'd to the Physicians* (1737), which draws upon *The Dispensary* for much of its tone, its medico-scatology, and its comic prophecies. The author of *Tom K[in]g's: Or, the Paphian Grove* (1738)—a mock-heroic poem about a battle between prostitutes—invokes the spirit of Garth to inspire his pen:

> . . . thou who Sung in an immortal Strain,
> The licens'd Homicides of *Warwick-Lane:*
> Give energy to my unskilful Tongue,
> While furious *Fanny's* direful rage is Sung.[22]

Likewise, Bonnell Thornton figuratively describes his mock-epic *The Battle of the Wigs* (1768) as an additional canto to *The Dispensary;* and in the preface to *The Lousiad* "Peter Pindar" (John Wolcot) refers to Garth as his distinguished forerunner, while the poem itself shows a distinctly Garthian strain in its imagery, descriptions, and use of allegorical figures."[23]

Unfortunately, what is probably the most significant part of Garth's impact upon eighteenth-century British poetry is not easily resolvable into a simple inventory of lines copied or influence acknowledged. For Garth's largest contribution may well consist of his central role in helping to establish the mock-heroic mode in Augustan satire. In the latter seventeenth century, the enormous popularity of Samuel Butler's *Hudibras* (1663-1678) had inaugurated a fashion for the "low" burlesque, in which serious subjects were lampooned by deliberately coarse diction, metrics, and imagery. Although Dryden, in his criticism and in his verse, had brilliantly urged the advantages of the polished mock-heroic mode, it remained for Garth to demonstrate those advantages in the first fully conceived, extended comic epic in the English language. "It is a Dispute among the Criticks," Addison writes in *The Spectator*, No. 249 (December 15, 1711), "whether Burlesque Poetry runs best in Heroic Verse, like that of the Dispensary, or in Doggerel, like that of *Hudibras*."[24] But even as these lines were being written, the critical dispute in question was being decided in favor of the Garthian "high" burlesque Addison himself favored. Eventually, most poets and critics would agree, and the mock-heroic emerged as the fundamental and most characteristic Augustan approach to satire—a result for which *The Dispensary*, both in its own right and through its formative influence on Pope, can justifiably claim much credit.

III *Garth's Latter-Day Reputation*

If by the end of the eighteenth century there were few critics willing to place Garth among the major poets, by the same token there were few who thought his achievement negligible. As an author who had successfully attracted readers, admirers, and imitators over the course of an entire century, Garth seemed to have fairly earned a secure and honorable position somewhere in the second rank of Augustan satirists. But with the advent of romanticism and its attendant reassessment of earlier literary reputations, Garth's precipitate decline into obscurity began. For as might be expected in an age when poets like Dryden and Pope fell into critical disfavor, a lesser figure like Garth all but disappeared from serious consideration.

During most of the nineteenth century Garth, if he was not altogether ignored, was seldom assigned more than the barest historical interest, as in Henry Hallam's *Introduction to the Literature of Europe* (1854): "In the year 1699, a poem was published, Garth's Dispensary, which deserves attention, not so much for its own merit . . . as from its indicating a transitional state in our versification. . . ."[25] Still more dismissive is Edmund

Gosse, who in 1889 wrote that "The fun has all faded out of *The Dispensary*, and Garth is no longer in the least degree attractive."[26] In 1884 John Dennis professed himself mystified at *The Dispensary*'s former popularity: "Few modern readers . . . will appreciate the welcome it received, and it is ludicrous to read in [Robert] Anderson's [1793] edition of the poet [cited earlier] that the poem 'is only inferior in humour, discrimination of character, and poetical ardour to the *Rape of the Lock.*' It would be far more accurate to say that the *Dispensary* has not a single merit of any kind."[27] By 1899, William Courthope could write—with the air of a man enunciating the obvious—that "Garth was utterly lacking in the gifts which alone could have made [his poem] permanently entertaining. . . . [*The Dispensary*] can only claim to be remembered to-day through a few hints that it appears to have given to the author of *The Dunciad.*"[28] In the face of such general agreement among Victorian critics, George Saintsbury's insistence on Garth's artistry (see chapters 2 and 3) seemed the merest eccentricity.

In our own day there are signs that Garth's reputation is enjoying at least a modest recovery from its nineteenth-century nadir. Like other literary figures of his era, Garth has benefitted from the general twentieth-century revival of interest in Augustan literature. The number of articles and dissertations dealing with Garth, though not large, has grown over recent decades, and most literary historians now readily agree with Austin Warren's contention that Garth is "the most successful practitioner of satire between Dryden and Pope."[29] In a similar vein, Tillotson calls Garth "the most important poet connecting the mock-heroics of Boileau and Pope"[30]; and Ellis praises *The Dispensary* as "a minor classic in the mock-epic mode."[31]

One factor which possibly more than any other has interfered with the modern reader's appreciation of *The Dispensary* is the remoteness of the events and the personalities involved in the satire. Even today's eighteenth-century specialist is apt to be at something of a loss when confronted by so particularized a topic as the medical politics which inspired Garth's poem. As Bonamy Dobrée puts it: "It must be confessed that *The Dispensary* . . . is somewhat indigestible, though taken in small morsels it has a flavour. It is not only that the circumstances which produced it have now only the dimmest historical interest and that the characters of the actors elude us, but that . . . it is too long, too elaborate."[32] More succinct is George Sherburn, in whose opinion *The Dispensary* "is so topical that it is now unreadable."[33]

With regard to such charges, it is hard to deny that *The Dispensary*, to the extent that it is a polemical document, requires considerable explication to make it fully accessible to a present-day reader. Yet to call it "unreadable" on that basis is surely an exaggeration. To one degree or another, almost any social satire will necessarily involve purely contemporary events, personalities, and attitudes: whether such a work merits our attention has less to do with its topicality than with the quality of its author's art. If today *The Dispensary* seems more dated and obscure than a work like *The Dunciad*, the reason would seem to lie not in Pope's greater universality, but rather in his greater poetic talent. In any case, it is only the scholar who need concern himself with the minutiae of Garth's contemporary allusions: for purposes of enjoyment and understanding, the general reader requires little more than a brief introduction and a comparative handful of crucial annotations.[34] Doubtless one major reason *The Dispensary* has appeared so unreadably topical to some is that until very recently there has been no readily available edition to provide the necessary background information.[35] That situation has been remedied, however, by the publication in 1970 of Ellis's splendid edition of *The Dispensary*, and henceforth the historical remoteness of Garth's subject matter should no longer loom as a serious hindrance to reader comprehension.

With that comprehension, it seems reasonable to hope, will come an increased recognition that *The Dispensary* (in the words of Pat Rogers):

. . . deserves a better fate than its current tiny niche in the textbooks. It was revised on a number of occasions up to 1718, which makes it a natural target for essays in pedantic bibliography. And its array of disguised medical men, all involved in a parochial squabble over a public dispensing hospital, allows scholarship a ready escape-route into historical details. In fact the artistic merits of the poem warrant greater attention. Garth channels a devious baroque allegory into a more graceful fancy—an essential stage in the development from *Hudibras* to *The Rape of the Lock*. . . . The comic epic, like the town eclogue, makes a domestic, urban setting replay the action of a pastoral narrative. Garth is very good at playing this trick. He uses the classical terms of natural description to portray landscapes that are grotesque, surreal or malign. *The Dispensary* tails off in its last two cantos, but it

Garth's Influence and Reputation

affords plenty of lively set-pieces and bravura comedy. A pity that Garth did not write more in this vein.[36]

Only a few will wish to claim more for Garth, but no discerning reader would want to see him granted less.

Notes and References

Chapter One

1. The information from the Peterhouse Register is cited by William H. Cornog, "Sir Samuel Garth: A Court Physician of the 18th Century," *Isis*, 29 (1938), 30. Cornog's investigation confirmed that the Garth family was indeed from Durham, rather than from Yorkshire where for two centuries Garth's biographers had mistakenly placed it.
2. See Robert Surtees, *The History and Antiquities of the County Palatine of Durham* (London, 1816-1840), IV, 26.
3. William Munk, *The Roll of the Royal College of Physicians of London* (London, 1878), I, 498.
4. *Poems on Affairs of State: Augustan Verse 1660-1714*, vol. 6, *1697-1704*, ed. Frank H. Ellis (New Haven, 1970), p. 60.
5. *Eighth Report of the Royal Commission on Historical Manuscripts* (London, 1881), p. 231.
6. Quoted by Cornog, "Sir Samuel Garth," p. 31.
7. Historical Manuscripts Commission, *The Manuscripts of the House of Lords, 1702-1704* (London, 1910), V, 203.
8. *Eighth Report of Royal Commission*, p. 231.
9. *Biographia Britannica* (London, 1747-1766), III, 2131, as quoted by Frank H. Ellis, "Garth's Harveian Oration," *Journal of the History of Medicine*, 18 (1963), 10.
10. There are at least two earlier brief works which have sometimes been ascribed, without evidence, to Garth: (1) Two letters "To my Lady —— at the Bath," dated September 6 and 13, 1692, in Abel Boyer's *Letters of Wit, Politicks and Morality* (London, 1701), pp. 377-80; (2) *Uraniae Metamorphosis in Sydus . . . Written by a Doctor of Physick* (London, 1695).
11. British Museum Add. MSS., no. 4225 (Ayscough's Catalogue). This anonymous life of Garth may be dated internally as between 1737 and 1760.
12. Ellis, "Garth's Harveian Oration," p. 15. The English version of Garth's oration is from the James M. Osborn manuscript in the library of the Yale University Medical School. Ellis maintains that the Osborn manuscript, which contains revisions, represents Garth's final draft prior to translation into Latin.

13. Ibid., p. 16.
14. Ibid., p. 19.
15. *The Works of the English Poets*, ed. Alexander Chalmers (1810; reprint ed., New York, 1970), IX, 424; hereafter cited as *Works of Poets*.
16. *Poems on Affairs of State*, vol. 6, ed. Ellis, p. 149.
17. John Dryden, *The Critical and Miscellaneous Prose Works of John Dryden*, ed. Edmund Malone (London, 1800), I, i, 497.
18. *Works of Poets*, ed. Chalmers, IX, 429.
19. John Dryden, *Poems of John Dryden*, ed. James Kinsley (Oxford, 1958), IV, 1532.
20. *Works of Poets*, ed. Chalmers, XX, 429-30.
21. Samuel Johnson, *The Lives of the English Poets*, ed. George B. Hill (1905; reprint ed., New York, 1967), I, 391.
22. Quoted by William Harvey, "John Dryden's First Funeral," *Athenaeum*, October 22, 1904, p. 552.
23. Ned Ward, *The London Spy*, ed. Ralph Straus (London, 1924), pp. 425-26.
24. George Farquhar, *Complete Works of George Farquhar*, ed. Charles Stonehill (New York, 1967), II, 321.
25. *Fifth Report of the Royal Commission on Historical Manuscripts* (London, 1876), pp. 359-60.
26. Thomas Hearne, *The Remains of Thomas Hearne*, comp. John Bliss, revised John Buchanan-Brown (Carbondale, Ill., 1966), pp. 314-15.
27. See Philip Pinkus, *Grub Street Stripped Bare* (Hamden, Conn., 1968), pp. 124-25.
28. Quoted by William H. Irving, *John Gay's London* (Cambridge, Mass., 1928), p. 74.
29. Dryden, *Works*, I, i, 347ff.
30. See Robert J. Allen, *The Clubs of Augustan London* (Cambridge, Mass., 1933), p. 234.
31. Walter Harte, *An Essay on Satire* (London, 1730), intro. Thomas Gilmore, Augustan Reprint Society Publication no. 132 (Los Angeles, 1968), p. 20.
32. Quoted by Richard C. Boys, *Sir Richard Blackmore and the Wits* (1949; reprint ed., New York, 1969), pp. 48-49.
33. See Philip E. Roberts. "A Critical Edition of Garth's Dispensary" (Ph.D. diss., University of Edinburgh, 1966), p. xl.
34. For the best brief account of the origins and history of the Kit-Cat Club, see Allen, *Clubs of Augustan London*, pp. 35-54, 232-39.
35. Samuel Garth, "The Letters of Samuel Garth," ed. John F. Sena, *Bulletin of the New York Public Library*, 78 (1974), 81.
36. Ibid.

Notes and References

37. David Green, *Sarah Duchess of Marlborough* (New York, 1967), p. 20. Green does not identify the quotation or give its source.

38. *Wentworth Papers, 1705-1739*, ed. J. Cartwright (London, 1882), p. 313.

39. *Seventh Report of the Royal Commission on Historical Manuscripts* (London, 1879), p. 508. On at least one earlier occasion Garth received a similar gift from another powerful Whig figure. In 1707, as the *Egmont Papers* show, the duke of Devonshire presented Garth with a ring. See *Sixth Report of the Royal Commission on Historical Manuscripts* (London, 1878), VI, 507.

40. Alexander Pope, *The Poems of Alexander Pope*, vol. 4, *Imitations of Horace*, ed. John Butt (New Haven, Conn., 1961), p. 105.

41. George Sherburn, *The Early Career of Alexander Pope* (Oxford, 1934), p. 52.

42. Alexander Pope, *The Poems of Alexander Pope*, vol. 1, *Pastoral Poetry and An Essay on Criticism*, ed. E. Audra and A. Williams (New Haven, Conn., 1961), p. 72.

43. Ibid.

44. Joseph Spence, *Observations, Anecdotes, and Characters of Books and Men*, ed. James Osborn (Oxford, 1966), I, 44.

45. Alexander Pope, *The Correspondence of Alexander Pope*, ed. George Sherburn (Oxford, 1956), III, 81.

46. Ibid., III, 291.

47. Narcissus Luttrell, *A Brief Historical Relation of State Affairs* (Oxford, 1857), IV, 681.

48. Robert Dodsley, *London and Its Environs* (London, 1761), V, 191.

49. Garth's professional connection with Sloane goes back at least to 1696, when both men served on the Committee on Medicines of the Royal College of Physicians. In 1699 Garth and Sloane appeared as medical witnesses for the defense in a murder trial. See Albert Rosenberg, "The Sarah Stout Murder Case: An Early Example of the Doctor as an Expert Witness," *Journal of the History of Medicine*, 12 (January, 1957), 61-70.

50. See Albert Rosenberg, *Sir Richard Blackmore: A Poet and Physician of the Augustan Age* (Lincoln, Nebr., 1953), pp. 109-10.

51. Ibid., p. 110.

52. Ibid., p. 113. Garth had been Wharton's physician as early as 1703. Sir John Vanbrugh, writing to Tonson on July 30, 1703, reports: "My Lord Wharton was got to Holme Pierpoint in his way to York, and there fell very ill. . . . he would fain have gone on, but with much ado they prevail'd with him to go back to Winchington, where he writ to Dr. Garth to meet him; Dr. Sloan too went downe, and extream ill they found him on Satterday last. . . ." Vanbrugh goes on to describe how

Wharton's life was feared for, but by "Wensday Garth left him (he says) out of Danger." John Vanbrugh, *The Complete Works of Sir John Vanbrugh*, ed. Bonamy Dobrée and Geoffrey Webb (London, 1928), IV, 10-11. Garth's personal opinion of his aristocratic patient may be gathered from a remark in one of Jonathan Swift's letters. Writing to Charles Ford (February 13, 1724), Swift says with regard to the earl of Peterborough: "I apply to Him what Garth said to me of Ld Wharton; A fine Gentleman I vow to God, but he wants Probity" (Jonathan Swift, *The Letters of Jonathan Swift to Charles Ford*, ed. D. Nichol Smith [Oxford, 1935], p. 104).

53. Quoted by Boys, *Blackmore and the Wits*, p. 108.
54. *Works of Poets*, ed. Chalmers, IX, 453.
55. Ibid.
56. Theodor Schenk, *Sir Samuel Garth und seine Stellung zum komischen Epos* (Heidelberg, 1900), p. 25.
57. Garth, "Letters," p. 85.
58. Harvey Cushing, "Dr. Garth: The Kit-Kat Poet," *Bulletin of the Johns Hopkins Hospital*, 17, no. 178 (January, 1906), 14, n. 36.
59. British Museum Add. MSS., no. 4225 (Ayscough's Catalogue).
60. Historical Manuscripts Commission, *Clements Mss.*, LV, pt. viii, 251.
61. See John S. Farmer and W. E. Henley, *Dictionary of Slang and Colloquial English* (London, 1905), p. 135.
62. Cushing, "The Kit-Kat Poet," p. 14.
63. *Report of the Historical Manuscripts Commission* (London, 1899), XXIX, pt. vii, 17.
64. C. K. Eves, *Matthew Prior: Poet and Diplomatist* (New York, 1939), pp. 266-67.
65. Alexander Andrews, *The History of British Journalism* (1859; reprint ed., New York, 1968), II, 111. Garth's contributions to *The Medley*, which are not now specifically identifiable, do not seem to have been extensive.
66. *Report of the Historical Manuscripts Commission* (London, 1899), XXIX, pt. v, 56.
67. Ibid., 54.
68. Samuel Garth, *The Dedication for the Latin Edition of Lucretius . . . Written in the Year 1711, by Dr. Garth; and Now made English by Mr. Oldmixon* (London, 1714), p. 9. Garth offers a more outspoken view of Queen Anne in "On Her Majesty's Statue in St. Paul's Church-Yard" (ca. 1715), discussed in chapter 4.
69. Jonathan Swift, *Journal to Stella*, ed. Harold Williams (Oxford, 1948), I, 48, 51, 75. On August 22, 1711, Swift refers in passing to having seen Garth among the company at White's Coffee-House (I, 337).

70. Ibid., II, 415.
71. Ibid., II, 494.
72. Jonathan Swift, *The Works of Jonathan Swift*, ed. Sir Walter Scott (London, 1883), V, 417-18.
73. Some years later, Swift offered another comic disparagement of Garth in the brief "History of Poetry," an elaborate series of puns and word plays on the names of English authors. In this work (first published in 1726), Swift says of Garth: "The Author of the *Dispensary* has Writ nothing else valuable, and therefore is too small in the GARTH [i.e., girth]" (Jonathan Swift, *The Prose Works of Jonathan Swift*, ed. Herbert Davis [Oxford, 1937-1968], IV, 275). The context is joking, but the sentiment no doubt reflects Swift's real opinion.
74. George Berkeley, *The Works of George Berkeley, Bishop of Cloyne*, ed. A. A. Luce and T. E. Jessop (London, 1956), VIII, 67.
75. Winston S. Churchill, *Marlborough: His Life and Times* (London, 1947), p. 1020.
76. Garth, "Letters," p. 78.
77. Ibid., pp. 75-76.
78. Ibid., p. 79. The letter is undated, but must predate April 2, 1717, since Garth mentions the duchess of Newcastle, who married the duke on that date.
79. Pope, *Correspondence*, I, 309.
80. *A New Miscellany of Original Poems, On Several Occasions* (London, 1701), p. 103, st. 5.
81. *Report of the Historical Manuscripts Commission*, XXIX, pt. iv, 256.
82. *Report of the Historical Manuscripts Commission*, LVI, pt, ii, 422.
83. Ibid., p. 469.
84. Ibid., p. 488.
85. Ibid., pt. iii, 25.
86. Henry St. John, *The Works of Lord Bolingbroke* (London, 1844; reprint ed., 1967), II, 300.
87. Quoted by Cornog, "Sir Samuel Garth," p. 40.
88. Garth, "Letters," pp. 76-77.
89. *Report of the Historical Manuscripts Commission*, LVI, pt. vi, 556.
90. Garth, *Dedication to Lucretius*, p. 8.
91. George Granville, *The Genuine Works in Verse and Prose of the Right Honourable George Granville, Lord Lansdowne* (London, 1732), p. 47. Granville's esteem is another indication of how Garth's friendships sometimes survived political differences: Granville was a confirmed Tory.
92. *Musapaedia, or Miscellany Poems Never before Printed* (Lon-

don, 1719), p. 31. See Albert Rosenberg, "The Last Days of Sir Samuel Garth: A Footnote to a Pope Letter," *Notes and Queries*, 204 (1959), 274.

93. Jonathan Swift, *Correspondence of Jonathan Swift*, ed. Harold Williams (Oxford, 1965), IV, 325. Garth's sentiment may have derived from Francis Bacon's comment in his essay "Of Death": "A man would die, though he were neither valiant nor miserable, only upon a weariness to do the same thing so oft over and over" (*Essays*, ed. A. S. Gaye [Oxford, 1911], p. 22).

94. Spence, *Anecdotes*, I, 325-26.

95. Ibid., I, 209.

96. See Roberts, "Critical Edition," p. xlvi.

97. British Museum Add. MSS. no. 47128, f. V, 95. By way of additional evidence of Garth's reputation for irreligion, Egmont reports: "I remember when Miss Campion the famous Dancer on the Stage died, who was kept by the old D. of Devonshire, it was reported that she was in great aggonie for her unchast life. The Doctor who attended her [Garth] and to whom she did not conceal her inquietude bid her rest contented, for upon his honour there was neither a God nor future State" (ibid.).

98. Spence, *Anecdotes*, I, 344.

99. Berkeley, *Works*, IV, 112.

100. Ibid., IV, 56-57. That Berkeley got this story firsthand from Addison has been questioned, since when Garth and Addison died (the latter six months after the former), Berkeley was away in Italy. It is possible, however, that Addison conveyed the story in a letter since lost.

101. *Bodlean Ms Hearne*, CIV, 66.

102. Alexander Pope, *Poems of Alexander Pope*, vol. 6, *Minor Poems*, ed. N. Ault and J. Butt (New Haven, Conn., 1964); p. 129.

103. Pope, *Correspondence*, II, 25.

104. Spence, *Anecdotes*, I, 208-9.

105. Ibid., I, 209.

106. Warren F. Dwyer, "Profit, Poetry, and Politics in Augustan Translation: A Study of the Tonson-Garth *Metamorphoses* of 1717" (Ph.D. diss., University of Illinois, 1969), p. 345.

107. Rosenberg, "The Last Days of Sir Samuel Garth," p. 274.

108. Among other evidence of Garth's high reputation as a physician is the dedication "To the Learned and Ingenious Sir *Samuel Garth*, Knt." of an anonymous medical book concerned with *General Observations and Prescriptions in the Practice of Physick on Several Persons of Quality* (London, 1715). Garth's fame as a doctor survived his death. In *A Poetical Essay of Physick* (London, ca. 1735), Garth is singled out for praise. He also figures in *Siris in the Shades: A Dialogue Concerning Tar-Water; Between Mr. Benjamin Smith, Lately*

Deceased, Dr. Hancock, and Dr. Garth at Their Meeting Upon the Banks of the Styx (London, 1744). In this unsigned work, the ghosts of Mr. Smith (who has not been identified) and Dr. John Hancock (erstwhile prebendary of Canterbury) debate the medicinal virtues of tar-water. Unable to agree, they refer the issue to the ghost of Garth, who decisively presents the author's contention that tar-water is medically worthless. See Marjorie Nicolson and G. S. Rousseau, "Bishop Berkeley and Tar-Water," *The Augustan Milieu: Essays Presented to Louis A. Landa,* ed. H. K. Miller, E. Rothstein, and G. S. Rousseau (Oxford, 1970), pp. 125-27.

109. Richard Steele, *Richard Steele's Periodical Journalism, 1714-1716,* ed. Rae Blanchard (Oxford, 1959), p. 3. Five years earlier, in *The Tatler,* No. 78, Steele had used Garth as the model for "Hippocrates," a physician, of whom Steele remarks: "There is not a more useful man in a commonwealth than a good physician; and by consequence no worthier a person than he that uses his skill with generosity even to persons of condition, and compassion to those who are in want: which is the behaviour of Hippocrates, who shows as much liberality in his practice, as he does wit in his conversation and skill in his profession" (*The British Essayists,* ed. Alexander Chalmers [Boston, 1856], II, 256-57).

110. Thomas Killigrew, *Miscellanea Aurea* (London, 1720), p. 2.
111. Giles Jacob, *The Poetic Register* (London, 1723), II, 58.
112. Joseph Warton, *An Essay on the Genius and Writings of Alexander Pope* (London, 1806), II, 26.
113. Garth, "Letters," p. 84.
114. John Arbuthnot, *Life and Works of Dr. John Arbuthnot,* ed. G. A. Aitken (London, 1892), p. 250.
115. Ibid., p. 460.
116. J. Timbs, *Clubs and Club Life in London* (London, 1872), p. 52.
117. British Museum, Stowe MS. no. 751, f. 142.
118. Lady Mary Wortley Montagu, *The Complete Letters of Lady Mary Wortley Montagu,* ed. Robert Halsband (Oxford, 1965), I, 182.
119. Ibid., I, 182. n. Garth was a friend as well as a physician to the Montagus. In her correspondence (ibid., I, 90, 100) Lady Mary refers to attending a ball given by Garth, whom she elsewhere characterizes as "a very worthy" man. See Spence, *Anecdotes,* I, 304.
120. Boyer, *Letters of Wit,* p. 217.
121. John Lacy, *The Steeleids* (London, 1714), p. 28.
122. Daniel Kenrick, *A New Session of Poets, Occasion'd by the Death of Mr. Dryden* (London, 1700), p. 8.
123. Montagu, *Complete Letters,* I, 17.
124. Steele, *Periodical Journalism,* p. 3.
125. Spence, *Anecdotes,* I, 326.
126. British Museum Add. MSS. no. 4225 (Ayscough's Catalogue).

127. See Garth, "Letters," nos. 4, 6-8, 11-16, 23, 28.

Chapter Two

1. *The Charter and Bye-Laws of the Royal College of Physicians of London* (London, 1959), p. ix.
2. Quoted by C. R. B. Barrett, *The History of the Society of Apothecaries of London* (London, 1905), p. xxxvii.
3. See George N. Clark, *A History of the Royal College of Physicians of London* (Oxford, 1964), I, 274.
4. The society's prosperity during the Commonwealth is reflected in its contribution of £1,000 toward a loan of £10,000 to the king by the City of London in 1664. The entire sum was subscribed to by nine members. See Ashworth Underwood, *A History of the Worshipful Society of Apothecaries of London* (London, 1963), I, 110-11.
5. Manuscript *Annals of the Royal College of Physicians of London*, as quoted by Roberts, "Critical Edition," p. xi.
6. Underwood says that in 1660 the College of Physicians numbered fewer than thirty (*History of Worshipful Society*, I, 93). Frank H. Ellis, however, estimates that at the Restoration "the College had [about] eighty members . . ." ("The Background of the London Dispensary," *Journal of the History of Medicine*, 20 [1965], 198). The size of Ellis's figure is due, presumably, to his inclusion of candidates for membership as well as the actual fellows of the college. The original limitation of the college to thirty Fellows was revised upward to forty under Charles II and to eighty under James II. By 1700, according to Ellis, the college had grown to about 130 (ibid.). The size of the Society of Apothecaries is more difficult to ascertain, though it was always much larger than the college and seems to have grown more so as the seventeenth century progressed. Ellis cites three contemporary estimates of the number of apothecaries in London about 1700: the figures range from circa 400 to over 2,000, with the former guess probably the more accurate (ibid., 199).
7. Nathaniel Hodges, *Loimologia: or, An Historical Account of the Plague in London in 1665* (London, 1720), p. 23, quoted by Ellis, "Background," p. 201.
8. Ibid.
9. See Albert Rosenberg, "The London Dispensary for the Sick-Poor," *Journal of the History of Medicine*, 14 (1959), 45. For a more detailed discussion of the medical pamphlet war in this period, see Charles F. Mullett, "Physician Vs. Apothecary, 1669-1671: An Episode in an Age-Long Controversy," *Scientific Monthly*, 49 (1939), 558-65.
10. *Lex Talionis; sive Vindiciae Pharmacoporum: Or A Short Reply to Dr. Merrett's Book* (London, 1670), p. 9.
11. For a survey of medical charity available prior to the dispensary,

Notes and References

see George Rosen, "Medical Care and Social Policy in Seventeenth Century England," *Bulletin of the New York Academy of Medicine*, 29 (1953), 420-37.

12. Among the more important earlier works advocating increased medical charity were John Cooke's *Unum Necessarium: Or, the Poore Mans Case* (London, 1648), Robert Boyle's *Some Considerations Touching the Usefulness of Experimental Naturall Philosophy* (London, 1663), and the anonymous *Englands Wants: Or Several Proposals Probably Beneficial For England* (London, 1667).

13. Quoted by Roberts, "Critical Edition," pp. xviii-xix.

14. *The Accomplisht Physician, the Honest Apothecary, and the Skilful Chyrurgeon* (London, 1670), p. 84; quoted by Ellis, "Background," pp. 203-4. *The Accomplisht Physician* has sometimes been attributed to Christopher Merrett, but Ellis convincingly rejects that ascription (ibid., p. 204).

15. *Bellum Medicinale* (London, 1701), p. 3; quoted by Ellis, "Background," p. 197.

16. See Roberts, "Critical Edition," p. xix.

17. Barrett, *History of Apothecaries*, p. 116.

18. Ibid., p. 94.

19. *The Statutes of the Colledge of Physicians London* (London, 1693), pp. 187-91; quoted by Ellis, "Background," p. 205.

20. M. F. A. Montagu, *Edward Tyson* (Philadelphia, 1943), p. 317.

21. *The Present State of Physick & Surgery in London* (London, 1701), p. 9.

22. Ellis, "Background," p. 205.

23. Roberts, "Critical Edition," p. xxi.

24. Ibid.

25. Barrett, *History of Apothecaries*, pp. 111-12.

26. Underwood, *History of Worshipful Society*, I, 127-28.

27. Roberts, "Critical Edition," p. xxiii.

28. Rosenberg, "London Dispensary," p. 48.

29. From the English manuscript version of Garth's oration, as reproduced in Frank H. Ellis, "Garth's Harveian Oration," *Journal of the History of Medicine*, 18 (1963), 19.

30. *A Short Answer to a Late Book Entituled, Tentamen Medicinale* (London, 1705), p. 34, reports 13,192 prescriptions filled between February, 1698, and February, 1701, and 71,999 filled between February, 1701, and December, 1704. See Ellis, "Background," p. 210.

31. Barrett, *History of Apothecaries*, p. 117.

32. Underwood, *History of Worshipful Society*, I, 388.

33. Ward, *The London Spy*, ed. Straus, p. 129.

34. *Works of Poets*, ed. Chalmers, IX, 426. See n. 37 below.

35. It is sometimes complained that the conclusion of *The Dispensary* is too abrupt and that the poem "seems rather to cease than to end" —

Hugh Walker, *English Satire and Satirists* (1925; reprint ed., New York, 1963), p. 167. Perhaps one reason for the seeming inconclusiveness at the poem's end is Garth's awareness that the battle was far from over: the dispensary had been built, but the real problem (i.e., dissension within the College of Physicians) remained as unresolved as ever. It can be argued, however, that at least the *moral* action of the poem is effectively resolved by Harvey's speech which envisages the ultimate restoration of harmony. In this speech (as in David's at the end of Dryden's *Absalom and Achitophel*) the reader is provided with a kind of anticipatory denouement of a conflict still in progress.

36. For a useful discussion and definition of the various species of burlesque poetry, as well as a history of these forms in England, see Richmond P. Bond, *English Burlesque Poetry 1700-1750* (Cambridge, Mass., 1932).

37. Samuel Garth, "The Dispensary," in *Poems on Affairs of State*, vol. 6., ed. Ellis, *T.N.*, 745. This edition of *The Dispensary* uses the second edition (1699) as its copy text: Garth's extensive postsecond edition revisions and additions are included with the textual notes at the rear of the volume. All further references to the poem (hereafter inserted parenthetically) are to this edition. References to the main text will be by canto and line number; references to Garth's later revisions and additions (for which Ellis does not assign line numbers) will appear as: *T.N.* (for textual notes) with the number of the page on which the passage occurs.

I have chosen the Ellis text of *The Dispensary* for citation (in spite of the awkwardness entailed in referring to Garth's revisions) because of its impeccable scholarship and general availability. Since Ellis does not reprint the prefatory material to the poem (i.e., dedication, preface, and congratulatory verses by Charles Boyle, Christopher Codrington, Thomas Cheek, and Henry Blount), citation for this material, as well as for Garth's minor poems, will be from "The Poems of Sir Samuel Garth" in *The Works of the English Poets*, vol. 9, ed. Alexander Chalmers (see n. 34 above). The 1810 edition of this work was reissued by photo-process in 1970, thus offering the only twentieth-century appearance in print of Garth's lesser works. Beyond the Ellis and Chalmers editions of *The Dispensary*, the poem has been reprinted earlier in this century: *"The Dispensary": Kritische Ausgabe*, ed. Wilhelm J. Leicht (Heidelberg, 1905). I have not chosen Leicht's edition for citation, partly because of its numerous errors and partly because it is a rare book, not readily obtainable outside the largest libraries.

38. Garth's familiarity with *Le Lutrin* was, in all likelihood, with the French original, rather than with a translation. Prior to 1699 the only known English translations of Boileau's poem were (1) an unpublished

manuscript version of canto 1, dated 1678 and probably by John Oldham, (2) a translation of the first four cantos by "*N.O.*," published in 1682 and not reprinted until modern times, and (3) a very loose adaptation issued by John Crowne in 1692 as *The Daeneids*. For more information on these early translations of *Le Lutrin*, see A. F. B. Clark, *Boileau and the French Classical Critics in England, 1660-1830* (1925; reprint ed., New York, 1970), pp. 142-50.

39. J. A. W. Bennett, "Oxford in 1699," *Oxoniensia*, 4 (1939), 150.
40. *Works of Poets*, ed. Chalmers, IX, 425.
41. *Poems on Affairs of State*, vol. 6, ed. Ellis, p. 150.
42. Ibid., VI, 170. Garth's friends came to his defense against such charges. Abel Boyer, in *The English Theophrastus* (1702), satirizes a foolish critic who ludicrously maintains that "*Ben. Johnson* is a Pedant; *Dryden* little more than a tolerable Versifier; *Congreve* a laborious Writer; *Garth*, an indifferent imitator of *Boileau*" (*Essays on Wit*, intro. W. Earl Britton, Augustan Reprint Society Publication no. 7 [Los Angeles, 1947], p. 10). See also Pope's defense of Garth in *Essay on Criticism*, III, ll. 618-19. Even Defoe eventually had kinder words for Garth. In his *Vindication of the Press* (London, 1718), p. 18, Defoe refers appreciatively to "the fine Humour of *Garth*."
43. See Clark, *Boileau*, p. 159 n.
44. See James M. Osborn, "The First History of English Poetry," in *Pope and His Contemporaries: Essays Presented to George Sherburn*, ed. James Clifford and Louis Landa (New York, 1968), p. 250.
45. Warton, *Essay on Pope*, I, 211.
46. Boyer, *Letters of Wit*, pp. 217-18.
47. Voltaire, *Oeuvres Complètes* (Paris, 1821), XXXVII, 407-8.
48. Schenk, *Sir Samuel Garth*, p. 66.
49. Clark, *Boileau*, p. 159.
50. Ibid., pp. 158-68, contains a full account, with parallel passages, of Garth's borrowings from Boileau.
51. *Le Lutrin* references (hereafter included parenthetically in the text) are to Nicholas Boileau, *Oeuvres Complètes*, ed. Françoise Escal (Paris, 1966), pp. 187-222.
52. For further discussion of Dryden's influence upon Garth, see Steven R. Phillips, "Sir Samuel Garth, *The Dispensary* (1699): An Old Spelling Edition with Introduction and Historical Notes" (Ph.D. diss., University of Rochester, 1969), pp. 123-26, 137-40. Also see Sister Mary Cabrini (Weber), "The Neo-Classical Mock-Epic and Its Relation to Epic and Satire" (Ph.D. diss., University of California at Berkeley, 1960), pp. 179-83.
53. John Dryden, *Essays*, ed. W. P. Ker (New York, 1961), II, 106. All page references to the *Discourse* (hereafter included parenthetically in the text) are to this edition.

54. George Saintsbury, *Cambridge History of English Literature*, ed. A. W. Ward and A. R. Waller (Cambridge, 1933), IX, 201-2.

55. Dryden, *Poems,* ed. Kinsley, I, 221. Further quotations from Dryden's verse (line numbers given parenthetically in the text) are from this edition.

56. See also Garth's characterization of Colon (II, 74-86). Garth's satiric character sketches show yet another Dryden technique, though one too diffuse to lend itself to simple illustration by quotation. In their formal orations, Garth's antidispensarians often show the same self-congratulatory inversion of moral criteria that we find in the speeches of Flecknoe and Shadwell in *MacFlecknoe*.

57. In connection with Dryden's call for dignity and beauty in comic-heroic satire, it is worth raising a point sometimes misunderstood by modern readers. It is often assumed that the satirist, by applying the conventions of serious heroic verse to comic ends, means thereby to ridicule the epic form itself. In the minds of Dryden and most other Augustan satirists, it seems clear that no such ridicule was intended. The ironic contrast engendered by imposing a Homeric framework upon a conspicuously un-Homeric subject was not meant to diminish Homer, but rather to emphasize how far from his ideal standards a unheroic age had fallen. Moreover, it was felt that the devices and language of heroic poetry, aside from their ironic function, could serve to add grace and dignity to a poem which, given its subject matter, might otherwise be merely sordid. As Walter Harte says of *"Epic Satire"* in his *Essay on Satire* (Augustan Reprint Society Publication no. 132 [Los Angeles, 1968], p. 6:

> The *common Dulness* of mankind, array'd
> In pomp, here lives and breathes, a *wond'rous Maid:*
> The Poet decks her with each unknown Grace,
> Clears her dull brain, and brightens her dark face.

Yet it should be pointed out that whatever the declared *intentions* of the satirists may have been, in practice the mock-heroic mode often did operate, if only peripherally, at the expense of the serious epic; for when elevated language and poetic conventions are inappropriately applied, they can hardly help but appear somewhat absurd in themselves. In this sense, Garth and the others who helped create the vogue for mock-epics may be said to have inadvertently contributed to the decline in prestige which the epic form was to suffer later in the century.

58. See Bond, *English Burlesque Poetry*, p. 56.

59. Ibid., p. 72.

Notes and References

Chapter Three

1. Johnson, *Lives of Poets,* ed. Hill, II, 60.
2. W. J. Courthope, *A History of English Poetry* (London, 1925), V, 55. Likewise, Guy L. Diffenbaugh, "The Rise and Development of the Mock Heroic Poem in England from 1660-1714" (Ph.D. diss., University of Illinois, 1926), p. 166, remarks that the subject of *The Dispensary* "was not trivial."
3. *Works of Poets,* ed. Chalmers, IX, 425-26.
4. Samuel Garth, "The Dispensary," III, 226, in *Poems on Affairs of State,* vol. 6, ed. Ellis. For an explanation of citations of *The Dispensary* (hereafter included parenthetically in the text) see chapter 2, n. 37.
5. Where the information seems pertinent, the names of the actual persons on whom Garth's characters are based are given in the text. For quick reference, however, it may be useful to include here a brief key to the major historical personages represented in *The Dispensary.* Apothecaries: Colon—Samuel Birch(?); Horoscope—Francis Bernard(?); Diasenna—Peter Gelsthorpe(?); Colocynthis—Thomas Gardiner; The Elder Ascarides—Michael Pierce; The Younger Ascarides—Edward Pierce. Apothecaries Physicians: Mirmillo—Dr. William Gibbons; Querpo—Dr. George Howe; Carus—Dr. Edward Tyson; Umbra—Dr. William Gold; The Bard—Sir Richard Blackmore. Physicians: Machaon—Sir Thomas Millington; Stentor—Dr. Charles Goodall; Celsus—Dr. John Bateman; Chiron—Dr. Thomas Gill.
6. Phillips, "Sir Samuel Garth, *The Dispensary* (1699): An Old Spelling Edition," p. 143.
7. Ibid., p. 142.
8. *Works of Poets,* ed. Chalmers, IX, 426.
9. For other Garth echoes of the classical epic, see Roberts, "Critical Edition," annotations, pp. 131ff.
10. It will be recalled that when Pope added the Rosicrucian machinery to his second version of *The Rape of the Lock,* "the scheme of adding it was much liked and approved by several of my friends, and particularly by Dr. Garth . . ." (J. Spence, *Observations,* ed. Osborn, I, 44).
11. See Bond, *English Burlesque Poetry,* p. 37.
12. Joseph Addison and Richard Steele, *The Spectator,* ed. Donald F. Bond (Oxford, 1965), II, 564.
13. Bond, *English Burlesque Poetry,* p. 156.
14. In this connection, it is significant that Garth's contemporaries were very often quite uncertain as to which persons the individual portraits in *The Dispensary* might be applied. In the various published and manuscript "keys" to the poem there is general agreement on only

a handful of identifications. So little individualized are Garth's portraits that even with the help of his own partial "key" (included as part of a letter to Arthur Charlett, master of University College, Oxford), the originals of such important characters as Colon and Horoscope remain in doubt. See *Poems on Affairs of State,* vol. 6, ed. Ellis, notes for II, lines 74 and 90. For the letter to Charlett, see Garth, "Letters," 93-94.

15. Johnson, *Lives of the Poets,* ed. Hill, II, 63-64. In offering this opinion, Johnson indicates his concurrence with a similar sentiment expressed by Jean du Resnel in *Les Principes de la Morale* (Paris, 1737).

16. John Dennis, *The Critical Works of John Dennis,* ed. E. N. Hooker (Baltimore, 1939-1943), II, 201.

17. The universality of Garth's portrait of Horoscope has led one modern critic to call Horoscope "a worthy successor to Sidrophel"—i.e., the greedy astrologer in Samuel Butler's *Hudibras.* See W. P. Jones, *The Rhetoric of Science* (Berkeley, Calif., 1966), p. 69.

18. *Works of Poets,* ed. Chalmers, IX, 425.

19. Warton, *Essay on Pope,* I, 213.

20. Alexander Pope, *The Poems of Alexander Pope,* vol. 2, ed. Geoffrey Tillotson (New Haven, Conn., 1966), 113.

21. George Campbell, *The Philosophy of Rhetoric,* ed. Lloyd F. Bitzer (Carbondale, Ill., 1963), p. 13.

22. *Gray's Inn Journal,* No. 50 (September 6, 1754), as quoted in Bond, *English Burlesque Poetry,* p. 54.

23. Ian Jack, *Augustan Satire: Intention and Idiom in English Poetry, 1660-1750* (Oxford, 1964), p. 85, n. Jack's opinion, however, is not shared by another modern critic, who writes: "Perhaps if Garth had included more purely descriptive passages . . . the poem might have better survived the passage of time" (John F. Sena, "Samuel Garth's *The Dispensary," Texas Studies in Literature and Language,* 15 [1974], 648).

24. In the deliberate "elevation" of his descriptive passages, Garth is not only following general contemporary poetic practice, but also the advice of his mentor, Boileau, who specifically urges the poet: "Soyez riche et pompeux dans vos descriptions. / C'est-là qu'il faut des vers étaler l'élegance" (*L'Art Poétique,* III, 258-59).

25. With regard to *The Dispensary's* action and plot, critics have widely differed. In Clark's opinion, "there is extremely little narrative in *The Dispensary;* we are kept waiting through four cantos for the action to begin" (Clark, *Boileau,* p. 159). Similarly, Bond complains that "The action of the poem is hardly excessive . . ." (Bond, *English Burlesque Poetry,* p. 156). Tillotson, on the other hand, contends that the poem suffers from "too many incidents" (*Poems of Pope,* II, 112). The apparent contradictions, however, may be only verbal, arising from the different ways in which such imprecise terms as "action" and "incident" are used. In discovering too little action in the poem, Clark

Notes and References

and Bond evidently refer only to the relative paucity of events. And when Tillotson finds the poem overcrowded with "incidents," he seems to include under that term not merely narrative occurrences, but also descriptive vignettes, philosophical observations, moral sentiments, and the like; and with these the poem is indeed oversupplied.

26. *Works of Poets*, ed. Chalmers, IX, 429.
27. Quoted in John Nichols, *Illustrations of the Literary History of the Eighteenth Century* (London, 1817), II, 764.
28. Edward Bysshe, *The Art of English Poetry*, (London, 1702).
29. *Works of Poets*, ed. Chalmers, IX, 429.
30. Johnson, *Lives of the Poets*, ed. Hill, II, 63.
31. Clark, *Boileau*, p. 415.
32. George Saintsbury, *The English Poets: Selections With Critical Introductions by Various Writers*, ed. Thomas H. Ward (London, 1885), III, 13. Elsewhere, in the course of a discussion of Pope's facility with heroic couplets, Saintsbury writes: "But something like it [i.e., Pope's skill] was hit earlier by Garth, the ingenious author of *The Dispensary* . . . , a man apparently of equal talent and merit . . ." (George Saintsbury, *The Peace of the Augustans* [London, 1916], p. 6).
33. Joseph Spence, "Quelques Remarques Hist.," as quoted by Osborn, "First History of English Poetry," *Pope and His Contemporaries*, ed. Clifford and Landa, p. 250.
34. George Saintsbury, *The History of English Prosody* (London, 1908), II, 449.
35. Johnson, *Lives of the Poets*, ed. Hill, II, 64. Johnson's measured praise takes on additional weight when viewed against his generally unenthusiastic response to *The Dispensary*. Despite his approval of the poem's moral position and its technical facility, he found "few lines . . . eminently elegant. No passages fall below mediocrity, and few rise much above it" (ibid., p. 63). So grudging did Johnson's praise of Garth seem to Horace Walpole, that he complained to William Mason (in a letter of February 19, 1781) of how "the tastless pedant . . . says that *The Dispensary*, that *chef-d'oeuvre*, can scarce make itself read . . . , but Dr. Johnson has indubitably neither taste nor ear, criterion of judgment, but his old woman's prejudices; where they are wanting, he has no rule at all" (Horace Walpole, *Correspondence*, ed. R. W. Lewis [New Haven, 1937-1973], XXIX, 111). Whatever his reservations about the poem, Johnson respected it enough to quote from it approvingly in his *Dictionary* and in his review of Soames Jenyns's *Free Inquiry into the Nature and Origin of Evil* (1757). Likewise, when Johnson entered Oxford as an undergraduate, among his small store of personal books was a copy of Garth's poem. See Aleyn L. Reade, *Johnsonian Gleanings* (1926; reprint ed., New York, 1968), V, 228.
36. Pope, *Poems*, vol. I, ed. Audra and Williams, ll. 350-51.

37. For a full record of Garth's revisions, see *Poems on Affairs of State*, vol. 6, ed. Ellis, pp. 722-50.
38. Jonathan Richardson, *Richardsoniana* (London, 1776), I, 195.
39. Saintsbury, *The Cambridge History of English Literature*, ed. Ward and Waller IX, 201. For other opinions in praise of Garth's revisions, see Richardson Pack, *Miscellanies in Verse and Prose* (London, 1719), pp. 96-97, and Henry Hallam, *An Introduction to the Literature of Europe* (New York, 1863), IV, pp. 239-40.
40. Killigrew, *Miscellanea Aurea*, p. 32.
41. In Pope, *Correspondence*, ed. Sherburn, II, 398.
42. *Poems on Affairs of State*, vol. 6, ed. Ellis, p. 723.
43. Richard Steele, *The Correspondence of Richard Steele*, ed. Rae Blanchard (Oxford, 1968), p. 436.
44. Oliver Goldsmith, *The Collected Works of Oliver Goldsmith*, ed. Arthur Friedman (Oxford, 1966), V, 324.
45. Johnson, *Lives of the Poets*, ed. Hill, II, 64.
46. Thomas B. Macaulay, *The Works of Lord Macaulay*, ed. Lady Trevelyan (Philadelphia, 1910), XVII, 10.
47. R. C. Jebb, *The Dictionary of National Biography*, ed. Leslie Stephen and Sidney Lee (Oxford, 1921-1922), II, 310.
48. H. W. Garrod, "Phalaris and Phalarism," in *Seventeenth Century Studies Presented to Sir Herbert Grierson* (Oxford, 1938), p. 369.
49. For the best study of the ancients-moderns controversy, see Richard F. Jones, "Ancients and Moderns: A Study of the Background of *The Battle of the Books*," *Washington University Studies*, n.s., *Language and Literature*, no. 6 (St. Louis, 1936).
50. The most famous of Boyle's literary defenders was Swift, to whom Bentley was one of those who "purchase Knowledge at the Expence / Of common Breeding, common Sense" (Jonathan Swift, "Ode to Sir William Temple," in *Poems*, ed. Harold Williams [Oxford, 1958], I, 27). In *The Battle of the Books*, Swift describes how Boyle allegorically impales the hapless Bentley on "a Launce of wondrous Length and sharpness"—i.e., Boyle's answer to Bentley's *Dissertation*. See Swift, *Works*, ed. Davis, I, 164-65. Similarly, in the "Apology" to *A Tale of a Tub*, Swift (using much the same metaphor Garth had employed) points out that many a fine work has resulted when some "*great Genius* [has thought] *it worth his while to expose a foolish Piece; . . . so the Earl of Orrery's Remarks will be read with Delight, when the Dissertation he exposes will neither be sought nor found*" (ibid., I, 5).
51. *Works of Poets*, ed. Chalmers, IX, 429.
52. Aside from Garth's tributes to William, the most sustained passages of individual praise in *The Dispensary* are those directed to Lord Somers (VI, 257-74), to Sir Thomas Millington (V, 141-46), and to Queen Anne (*T.N.*, 731)—the latter lines being added to the fifth

Notes and References

edition in 1703 after Anne's accession to the throne. In contrast to the length and luxuriance of his eulogies of William, Garth's three meager couplets on Anne seem little more than the minimum obligatory politeness due to any reigning monarch. Even Garth's eighteen lines of panegyric to Lord Somers may be construed as partly in praise of William; for at the time of writing, Somers was serving as lord chancellor, in which office, Garth makes clear, he was the agent of "Heav'n and the Great *Naussau*" (VI, 258).

53. *The Dissertator in Burlesque* (London, 1701), p. 7, quoted in Bond, *English Burlesque*, p. 243.
54. Sir Richard Blackmore, "A Satyr Against Wit," *Poems on Affairs of State*, vol. 6, ed. Ellis, p. 143.
55. As cited by Clark, *Boileau*, p. 159.
56. Bond, *English Burlesque Poetry*, p. 156.
57. Karlernst Schmidt, *Vorstudien zu einer Geschichte des Komischen Epos* (Saale, 1953), p. 94.
58. *Works of Poets*, ed. Chalmers, IX, 430.

Chapter Four

1. William Coward, *Licentia Poetica Discuss'd: Or, The True Test of Poetry* (London, 1709), p. 25.
2. *Works of Poets*, ed. Chalmers, IX, 425.
3. John Gay, *The Letters of John Gay*, ed. C. F. Burgess (Oxford, 1966), p. 23.
4. On August 11, 1715, Pelham-Holles became the duke of Newcastle, by which title he is most often designated. When Garth came to know him, Newcastle was at the start of his contentious and influential political career. Unfortunately Garth did not live long enough to reap the full benefits of so impressive a connection.
5. Johnson, *Lives of the Poets*, ed. Hill, I, 77.
6. *Works of Poets*, ed. Chalmers, IX, 447. All references to *Claremont* and to Garth's occasional poems (hereafter included parenthetically in the text) are to this edition.
7. Ibid., IX, 446.
8. Ibid.
9. Ibid., XX, 421.
10. *The Gentleman's Magazine*, 2 (1732), 1122.
11. Cornog, "Sir Samuel Garth," p. 39. Cornog does not elaborate on his opinion.
12. [Robert Shiells], (Theophilus Cibber is given as author), *The Lives of the Poets of Great Britain and Ireland* (London, 1753), IV, 267.
13. Establishing the precise canon of Garth's occasional verse is difficult, since, like most poets of his day, he did not always acknowledge his more ephemeral works. Moreover, it was a common

practice of the time for publishers of poetic miscellanies to give a list of contributors (sometimes spurious) on the title page, without any further indication of which works belonged to which authors. For a checklist of those works which may confidently be assigned to Garth, see Roberts, "Critical Edition," pp. lvi-lvii.

14. Swift, *Works*, ed. Scott, V, 418. A more ingenious explanation for the alleged deterioration of Garth's poetic skills is found in the anonymous "Brooke and Hellier" (1712), which laments a law forbidding the importation of certain French wines. One result of this law, it seems, was a sharp decline in poetic inspiration. "Had not our liquor been so foul,/How could bright Garth have e'er been dull." See Irving, *John Gay's London*, p. 124.

15. Boys, *Blackmore and the Wits*, p. 62.

16. Ibid., pp. 74-75. Blackmore's irritation is understandable, since almost without exception the poems in the *Commendatory Verses* had disparaged his medical abilities. The preface to the *Discommendatory Verses* (written either by Blackmore or under his direction) wearily complains that the wit of the anti-Blackmoreans consists mostly of variations on such "excellent Rhimes" as *"Bills, Pills,* and *Kills"* (ibid., p. 66). In this connection, however, it is worth noting that while Garth does not use these rhymes in "To the Merry Poetaster," "pill" and "kill" *do* show up in Blackmore's rejoinder, "To the Sorry Poetaster."

17. See Bruce Harris, *Charles Sackville, Sixth Earl of Dorset: Patron and Poet of the Restoration* (Urbana, Ill., 1940), p. 220. For a further account of the Kit-Cat toasting tradition, see Joseph Addison, *Tatler*, No. 24. (June 2-4, 1709).

18. Norman Moore, "The Life of Garth," in *The Dictionary of National Biography*, ed. Stephen and Lee, VII, 910.

19. In 1734 John Ralph rewrote the Vanbrugh et al. adaptation and called it *The Cornish Squire*. Ralph retained the Garth prologue, which has sometimes since been called the "Prologue to *The Cornish Squire.*"

20. See Robert J. Allen, "The Kit-Cat Club and the Theater," *Review of English Studies*, 7 (1931), 56-61.

21. Ibid., p. 58. Daniel Defoe likewise denounced the "Vice and Prophaneness" of Garth's prologue, See Daniel Defoe, *The Review* (Facsimile Text Society, New York, 1938), 4, 102.

22. Pope, *Correspondence*, ed. Sherburn, I, 175.

23. Macaulay, *Works*, ed. Trevelyan, XVI, 150.

24. Mary E. Knapp, *Prologues and Epilogues of the Eighteenth Century* (New Haven, Conn., 1961), p. vii.

25. *British Essayists*, ed. Chalmers, XIII, 228.

26. A political poem often attributed to Garth is "To the Duke of Marlborough, On His Voluntary Banishment" (1712). Recently, however, it has been shown that the author is Dr. George Sewell. See

Notes and References

Albert Rosenberg, "The Authorship of the Verses on Marlborough's Exile," *Notes and Queries*, 201 (1956), 429-30.

27. Matthew Prior, *The Literary Works of Matthew Prior*, ed. H. B. Wright and M. K. Spears (Oxford, 1971), I, 389. Prior had started his career as a Whig, and as such had been a member of the Kit-Cat Club. Garth admired Prior, who had been his contemporary at Cambridge, and in *The Dispensary* he tells us that "what *Apollo* dictates, *Prior* sings" (IV, 227). However, when Prior switched his allegiance from Whig to Tory, he was expelled from the Kit-Cats, and his friendship with Garth went by the boards. It would seem, however, that Garth took no great personal offense at Prior's attack in *The Examiner*, since he did not remove the lines praising Prior from later editions of *The Dispensary*. After the Whig triumph of 1714, Prior was for a time imprisoned for his role as a Tory diplomat. He was released under the 1717 Act of Grace, and when he decided to publish a volume of his poems in 1719, one of the first subscribers was Dr. Samuel Garth. See Johnson, *Lives of the Poets*, ed. Hill, II, 194, n.

28. Prior, *Works*, ed. Wright and Spears, I, 393.

29. Joseph Addison, *The Works of Joseph Addison*, ed. G. W. Greene (New York, 1860), II, 595.

30. *British Essayists*, ed. Chalmers, IV, 254.

31. Johnson, *Lives of the Poets*, ed. Hill, II, 61.

32. C. W. Previté-Orton, *Political Satire in English Poetry* (Cambridge, 1910), p. 126. Although this poem was written when Anne was dead and (at least to the Whigs) partly discredited, it still required considerable boldness on Garth's part to be so outspoken about so recent a monarch. In the British Library there is a contemporary manuscript copy of Garth's poem, to which someone—presumably a Whig—has added the superscription: "They say for this the Author's like to rue, / 'Tis something harsh, but not so harsh as true." See British Museum, Add. MS. no. 35335, f. 30.

33. John Gay, *Poetry and Prose*, ed. Vinton Dearing (Oxford, 1974), I, 40. See also Gay's reference in *Trivia*, II, 564: "And *Squirts* read *Garth*, 'till Apozems [medical infusions] grow cold" (ibid., I, 159).

34. A Latin poem that has been attributed to Garth is *Uraniae Metamorphosis in Sydus: Or The Transfiguration of Our Late Glorious Sovereign Queen Mary* (1695). This work is listed under "Garth" in the British Library (press mark 11630 g. 41–17), though there seems no basis for the ascription other than the tenuous facts that the author is identified as a "Doctor of Physick" who in his preface says he is little accustomed to writing verse.

35. *Fifth Report of the Royal Commission on Historical Manuscripts* (London, 1876), pp. 359-60.

36. Hearne, *Remains*, comp. Bliss, revised Buchanan-Brown, p. 315.

37. *The Poets of Great Britain Complete from Chaucer to Churchill,* ed. John Bell (Edinburgh, 1779); quoted by Schenk, *Sir Samuel Garth,* p. 7.

38. Samuel Garth, *Oratio Laudatoria, In Aedibus Collegii Regalis Med. Lond.* (London, 1697). To the printed version of his lecture Garth added a dedication to Charles Montagu (later Lord Halifax), who was then first lord of the treasury and president of the Royal Society. In his dedication Garth praises Halifax as a "Viro Amplissimo, Ornatissimo." Halifax prided himself on his literary taste, and William Shippen, in *Faction Display'd* (1704) suggests that Halifax "help'd to Polish Garth's rough, awkward Lays" (*Poems on Affairs of State,* vol. 6, ed. Ellis, p. 665). A more convincing picture of Halifax's literary relationship with Garth is found in a story told by Pope. While working on his translation of *The Iliad,* Pope read some of his efforts to Halifax, who responded with a number of vague criticisms. "I returned from Lord Halifax's with Dr. Garth in his chariot, and . . . was saying to the Doctor that my Lord had laid me under a good deal of difficulty by such loose and general observations. . . . Garth laughed heartily at my embarrassment, said I had not been long enough acquainted with Lord Halifax to know his way yet. . . . 'All you need do,' says he, 'is to leave [the criticized passages] just as they are, call on Lord Halifax two or three months hence . . . and then read them to him as altered. I have known him much longer than you have, and will be answerable for the event. . . .'" Pope followed Garth's advice, and Halifax, as predicted, professed to find the passages much improved. See Spence, *Observations,* I, 87-88.

39. Munk, *Roll of the Royal College of Physicians,* III, 360-61.
40. Garth, *Oratio,* p. 1.
41. See Ellis, "Garth's Harveian Oration," pp. 8-19.
42. Ibid., p. 13.
43. Garth, *Oratio,* pp. 3-4.
44. Johnson, *Lives of the Poets,* ed. Hill, II, 60.
45. Samuel Garth, *The Dedication for the Latin Edition of Lucretius* (London, 1714), p. 1.
46. *La Critique Histoire de la République des Lettres* (Paris, 1713), II, 284, as quoted by Wolfgang B. Fleischmann, *Lucretius and English Literature, 1680-1740* (Paris, 1964), p. 75.
47. Ibid., pp. 75-76. Lucretius does not seem to have been a favorite of Garth's. Aside from *The Dedication*—where the Latin author is called "Eruditat ne utilius an delectet elegantius" (*Dedication,* p. 1)— Garth's only other direct allusion is in the preface to Ovid's *Metamorphoses,* where Lucretius, "though in other things most penetrating" (*Works of Poets,* ed. Chalmers, XX, 416), is criticized for his inaccurate description of the sun. In *The Dispensary* only a few passages reflect the influence of Lucretius, and one modern critic, after

surveying those, concludes that "the Lucretian-Epicurean imagery in the *Dispensary* is used in an unsympathetic manner" (Fleischmann, *Lucretius and English Literature*, p. 241). Given the paucity of Garth's allusions to Lucretius, we can only wonder on what basis the editor of *La Critique Histoire de la République des Lettres* (cited earlier) credits him with "la réputation d'etre entré aussi avant, que personne dans les sentiments de cet ancien Epicurien" (ibid., p. 75).

48. Garth, *Dedication*, p. 1. Oldmixon's translation of this passage reads: "One must run the Hazard of being censur'd as Vain and Presumptuous that dares prefix so Great and August a Name to such an Inconsiderable Attempt; but I am as well sensible of Your Humanity as my own Incapacity" (ibid., p. 5).

49. [Shiells], *Lives of the Poets*, IV, 269.

50. In his letter to Vernon (dated November 22, 1715) Tonson explains that "the Encouragement of Sr Samuel Garth" lies behind his request" (British Museum, Stowe MS. 155, f. 97). Garth's letter to Vernon seconds the request, asking that Vernon "oblige mee to translate this inclos'd" (Garth, "Letters," p. 90). Sena, evidently unaware that the requested translation was for the Ovid edition, comments: "Presumably the enclosure was in Latin, which tends to give credence to those who thought that Garth was inept in that language" (ibid.).

51. Pope, *Poems*, vol. 6, ed. Butt, p. 172.

52. *Works of Poets*, ed. Chalmers, XX, 426.

53. Ibid., 416.

54. Ibid., 429. Garth's preface to Ovid was disparaged by Joseph Warton, who found it "written in a free and lively style, but full of strange opinions" (Warton, *Essay on Pope*, II, 25, n.). Likewise, Johnson considered the preface "written with more ostentation than ability: his notions are half-formed, and his materials immethodically confused" (Johnson, *Lives of the Poets*, ed. Hill, II, 62). Since neither Warton nor Johnson explains his remarks, it is not altogether clear just what in Garth's preface they find objectionable. The most likely targets would seem to be Garth's assumption that the *Metamorphoses* was an unrevised draft and his somewhat deistic account of the edifying moral lessons it contains.

55. Ibid.

56. Dwyer, "Profit, Poetry, and Politics," p. 253. Dwyer's study contains a full account of the background of the edition and an informed critical assessment of its quality as a translation.

57. Ovid, *Metamorphoses*, with an English Translation by Frank Justus Miller (Cambridge, Mass., 1968), II, 303, 305.

58. *Works of Poets*, ed. Chalmers, XX, 541-42.

59. Dwyer, "Profit, Poetry, and Politics," p. 254. However, to the contention that Garth eschews the "poetic" should be added Dwyer's

earlier complaint that in Garth's translation (as in those by Arthur Maynwaring, Nahum Tate, and Laurence Eusden) Ovid's "pathos and terror become progressively intensified" (ibid., p. 247).

60. Like so many classical translations of the period, the Garth *Metamorphoses* was in part intended as a party document, and some of the distortions Ovid suffered in this edition derived from conscious efforts to heighten and emphasize those passages and incidents that might be allegorically read as favorable to the Whigs. For a discussion of this aspect of the work, see ibid., pp. 259-333.

61. Douglas Bush, *Mythology and the Romantic Tradition in English Poetry* (Cambridge, Mass., 1937), pp. 24-25.

62. William H. Irving, *John Gay: Favorite of the Wits* (Durham, N.C., 1940), p. 12.

63. Dwyer, "Profit, Poetry, and Politics," p. 2.

64. F. Seymour Smith, *The Classics in Translation: An Annotated Guide to the Best Translations of the Greek and Latin Classics in English* (1930; reprint ed., 1968), p. 245. A further indication of the enduring appeal of the Garth *Metamorphoses* is its recent (1958) reissuance. See bibliography below.

65. L. P. Wilkinson, *Ovid Surveyed* (Cambridge, 1962), p. 223.

Chapter Five

1. *Poems on Affairs of State*, vol. 6, ed. Ellis, p. 710.

2. See Boys, *Blackmore and the Wits*, p. 49.

3. *Poems on Affairs of State*, vol. 6, ed. Ellis, p. 710, n.

4. Horace Walpole, *The Letters of Horace Walpole*, ed. Paget Toynbee (Oxford, 1905), XV, 111.

5. Charles Churchill, *The Poetical Works of Charles Churchill*, ed. Douglas Grant (Oxford, 1956), p. 143.

6. *The Gentleman's Magazine*, 9 (1739), 74.

7. William Ayre, *Memoirs of the Life and Writings of Alexander Pope, Esq.* (London, 1745), I, 304.

8. Vicesimus Knox, *Cursory Thoughts on Satire and Satirists* (London, 1778), as quoted by Clark, *Boileau*, p. 51.

9. William Hayley, *An Essay on Epic Poetry* (London, 1782), III, 461-64.

10. *The Works of the British Poets*, ed. Robert Anderson (Edinburgh, 1793), as quoted by John Dennis, *The Age of Pope: 1700-1744* (London, 1894), p. 96. Not everyone preferred Pope's poem to Garth's. In 1714 Charles Gildon disparaged *The Rape of the Lock* as inferior to both *The Dispensary* and *Le Lutrin*. See Bond, *English Burlesque Poetry*, pp. 75-76.

11. In Boys, *Blackmore and the Wits*, p. 108.

12. See Bond, *English Burlesque Poetry*, pp. 243-44.

13. Pope's copy of the fifth edition of *The Dispensary* is in the Forster Collection (3325) of the Victoria and Albert Museum, London. His copy of the sixth edition is in the Huntington Library (105684), San Marino, California.

14. Alexander Pope, *The Poems of Alexander Pope*, ed. John Butt (New Haven, Conn., 1950-1969), vol. 5, *The Dunciad*, ed. James Sutherland, pp. 113-14. All line references to Pope's poetry (hereafter included parenthetically in the text) are to this, the Twickenham Edition.

15. Ibid., 114, n.

16. Alexander Pope, *The Works of Alexander Pope*, ed. Elwin-Courthope (London, 1889), V, 433.

17. Pope, *Poems*, vol. 2, ed. Tillotson, p. 115. Tillotson also remarks that "Among the medical lumber of [Garth's] poem are satiric references to the 'beau monde' . . . that provide Pope with hints and materials" (ibid., p. 113).

18. *Poems on Affairs of State*, vol. 6, ed. Ellis, pp. 64-66. All line references to *The Dispensary* (hereafter included parenthetically in the text) are to this edition. See chapter 2, n. 37.

19. For a fuller discussion of parallel passages between these two works see Schenk, *Sir Samuel Garth*, pp. 85-96.

20. Jack, *Augustan Satire*, p. 85, n.

21. For other parallels between *The Dispensary* and *The Dunciad*, see Schenk, *Sir Samuel Garth*, pp. 96-107. Though heaviest in *The Rape of the Lock* and *The Dunciad*, Pope's borrowings from Garth were not limited to those works. Limitations of space do not allow a listing here of all such borrowings, but interested readers may wish to look up the following examples of the many that could be cited: *The Dispensary*, IV, 221-22 and *The Pastorals*, "Winter," ll. 11-12; *The Dispensary*, VI, 202-3 and *The Pastorals*, "Autumn," ll. 67-68; *The Dispensary*, VI, 120 and the translation of Statius' *Thebais*, l. 146; *The Dispensary*, VI, 28 and the translation of "The Episode of Sarpedon" from Homer's *The Iliad*, l. 220; *The Dispensary*, III, 34 and *The Essay on Criticism*, l. 430; *The Dispensary*, I, 140 and *The Essay on Man*, I, 140; and *The Dispensary*, IV, 60-61 and the translation of Homer's *The Iliad*, IX, 418-19.

22. In Bond, *English Burlesque Poetry*, p. 402.

23. Many other eighteenth-century authors, though not significantly influenced by Garth, nevertheless paid him the compliment of borrowing his lines. Among the many examples of this are: Garth's "And knows, that to be Rich is to be Wise" (II, 94) and Defoe's "Tells you how Wise he is; *that is, how Rich:/For Wealth is Wisdom; he that's Rich is wise*" ("The True-Born Englishman" [1701], ll. 591-92; in *Poems on Affairs of State*, vol. 6, ed. Ellis, p. 285); Garth's " 'Tis doubtful which is Sea, and which is Sky" (V, 176) and Swift's

" 'Twas doubtful which was Rain, and which was Dust" ("A Description of a City Shower" [1710], l. 126; in *The Poems of Jonathan Swift*, ed. Harold Williams [Oxford, 1958], I, 137); Garth's "And curling Sheets of Smoke obscure the Skies" (I, 100) and Gay's "And curling Clouds of Incense hide the Skies" ("The Fan" [1714], l. 62; in *Poetry and Prose*, ed. Dearing, I, 60); Garth's "Where little Villains must submit to Fate,/That great Ones may enjoy the World in state" (I, 9-10) and Gay's "For *petty rogues submit to fate / That great ones may enjoy their state*" ("Pythagoras and the Countryman" [1727], ll. 39-40; ibid., II, 350); and Garth's "Where Billows never break, nor Tempests roar "(*T.N.*, 736) and Cowper's "Where tempests never beat nor billows roar" ("On the Receipt of My Mother's Picture" [1790], l. 97; in *Poetical Works of William Cowper*, ed. H. S. Milford [London, 1967], p. 396).

24. Addison and Steele, *The Spectator*, ed. Bond, II, 468.

25. Hallam, *Introduction to the Literature of Europe*, IV, 239.

26. Edmund Gosse, *A History of Eighteenth Century Literature* (London, 1889), p. 34.

27. Dennis, *Age of Pope*, p. 96.

28. William J. Courthope, *The Life of Alexander Pope* (London, 1899), p. 106.

29. Austin Warren, *Alexander Pope as Critic and Humanist* (Princeton, N.J., 1929), p. 172.

30. Pope, *Poems*, II, ed. Tillotson, p. 112.

31. *Poems on Affairs of State*, vol. 6, ed. Ellis, p. vii. Somewhat more equivocal is Earl Miner, who (after commenting that except for Dryden's "no other great satire appeared between 1688 and the eighteenth century"), remarks: "Garth's *Dispensary* (1699) provides a single major exception, if it is major" (Earl Miner, *The Restoration Mode from Milton to Dryden* [Princeton, N.J., 1974], p. 456).

32. Bonamy Dobrée, *English Literature in the Early Eighteenth Century, 1700-1740* (Oxford, 1959), p. 129.

33. George Sherburn, in *A Literary History of England*, ed. A. C. Baugh (New York, 1948), p. 899. Similarly, Robert K. Root, in *The Poetical Career of Alexander Pope* (Princeton, N.J., 1941), p. 75, writes: "Though very acceptable to contemporary readers who knew of the quarrel and could identify the personalities, the *Dispensary*, despite the nervous vigour of its couplets, is for us today rather dull reading. Pope, doubtless, read it with keen zest."

34. Lester King, *The Medical World of the Eighteenth Century* (Chicago, 1958), p. 14, writes: "Loaded with mythological and classical allusions and contemporary references, [*The Dispensary*] is at first a little rugged for the modern taste. But after one or two readings the difficulties recede, and the modern reader can appreciate the

Notes and References

rollicking spirit and clever satire, especially if he ignores the more obscure references."

35. In the first two thirds of the twentieth century only one edition of the poem—Leicht's *Sir Samuel Garth's The Dispensary: Kritische Ausgabe mit Einleitung und Anmerkungen*—was published, and this edition was rendered doubly inaccessible to the average English-speaking reader by its rarity and the fact that all the notes and commentary are in German.

36. Pat Rogers, *The Augustan Vision* (New York, 1974), pp. 175-76. Elsewhere Rogers refers to *The Dispensary* as "a work once greatly admired—perhaps excessively so—and now, as is the way, unduly deprecated" (Pat Rogers, *Grub Street: Studies in a Subculture* [London, 1972], p. 36). In this sentiment Rogers echoes Hugh Walker, who writes that *The Dispensary* "certainly did not deserve the panegyrics of contemporaries; but perhaps the reaction has gone a little too far the other way" (Walker, *English Satire*, p. 167).

Selected Bibliography

PRIMARY SOURCES

1. Important editions of *The Dispensary*

The Dispensary: A Poem. London: John Nutt, 1699.
The Dispensary: A Poem in Six Cantos. 4th ed. London: John Nutt, 1700.
The Dispensary: A Poem in Six Cantos. 6th ed. London: John Nutt, 1706.
The Dispensary: A Poem in Six Cantos. 7th ed. London: Jacob Tonson, 1714.
The Dispensary: A Poem in Six Cantos. 8th ed. London: Jacob Tonson, 1718.
Garth's "Dispensary": Kritsche Ausgabe mit Einleitung und Anmerkungen. Edited by Wilhelm Leicht. Heidelberg: Carl Winter's Universitätsbuchhandlung, 1905. Marred by errors; based on the seventh edition (1714).
"A Critical Edition of Garth's *Dispensary*." Edited by Philip E. Roberts. Ph.D. dissertation, University of Edinburgh, 1966. Uses second edition (1699) as copy-text; excellent notes and background.
"Sir Samuel Garth, *The Dispensary* (1699): An Old Spelling Edition with Introduction and Historical Notes." Edited by Steven R. Phillips. Ph.D. dissertation, University of Rochester, 1969. Uses eighth edition (1718) as copy-text; useful and informative.
The Dispensary. In *Poems on Affairs of State: Augustan Satirical Verse 1660-1714*, vol. 6, *1697-1704*. Edited by Frank H. Ellis. New Haven: Yale University Press, 1970. Uses second edition (1699) as copy-text; a meticulous and knowledgeable job.
The Dispensary (1699) and *Claremont* (1715). Introduction by Jo Allen Bradham. Delmar, N.Y.: Scholars' Facsimile Reprints, 1975. Reproductions of the first editions.

2. Other writings

Oratio Laudatoria: In Aedibus Collegii Regalis Med. Lond. London: Abel Roper, 1697.
"Life of Otho." In *Plutarch's Lives: The Translation called Dryden's*. 5 vols. Edited by A. H. Clough. Historical notes by William Smith.

Selected Bibliography

New York: Bigelow, Brown & Co., 1911. Garth's "Otho" is in volume 5.

"The Second Philippick." In *Several Orations of Demosthenes . . . English'd from the Greek by Several Hands.* London: Jacob Tonson, 1702.

The Dedication for the Latin Edition of Lucretius . . . Written in the Year 1711 and Now Made English by Mr. Oldmixon. London: J. Roberts, 1714. Contains Garth's original Latin text as well as John Oldmixon's translation.

Claremont: Address'd to the Right Honourable the Earl of Clare. London: Jacob Tonson, 1715.

Ovid. *Metamorphoses in Fifteen Books: Translated into English Verse Under the Direction of Sir Samuel Garth.* Introduction by Gilbert Highet. Verona: Officina Bodini, 1958. Issued by the Limited Editions Club in honor of Ovid's bimillenial anniversary.

"The Letters of Samuel Garth." Edited by John F. Sena. *Bulletin of the New York Public Library,* 78 (1974), 69–94. Garth's thirty-one surviving letters.

"Poems." In *The Works of Celebrated Authors.* 2 vols. London: Tonson and Draper, 1750. *The Dispensary* and Garth's other verses are in volume 1.

"Garth's Poems." In *The Works of the English Poets.* 75 vols. Edited by Samuel Johnson. London: J. Buckland et al., 1790. *The Dispensary* and Garth's other verses are in volume 20.

"Works of Garth." In *The Works of the English Poets From Chaucer to Cowper.* 21 vols. Edited by Alexander Chalmers. London: J. Johnson et al., 1810; reprint ed., Hildesheim: Georg Olms, 1970. Garth's poetry is in volume 9. His edition of Ovid is in volume 20.

SECONDARY SOURCES

Anon. "Sir Samuel Garth." British Museum Add. MSS. no. 4225 (Ayscough's Catalogue). A biographical sketch dating from the mid-eighteenth century.

Boyce, Benjamin. *"The Dispensary,* Sir Richard Blackmore, and the Captain of the Wits." *Review of English Studies,* 14 (1938), 453–58. Discusses the response of Blackmore and others to *The Dispensary.*

Boys, Richard C. *Sir Richard Blackmore and the Wits.* 1949; reprint ed., New York: Octagon Books, 1969. Background of the *Commendatory Verses* and the *Discommendatory Verses,* with texts of both.

Cook, Richard I. "Garth's *Dispensary* and Pope's *Rape of the Lock.*"

C.L.A. Journal, 6 (1962), 107-16. Similarities and differences between the two discussed.

CORNOG, WILLIAM H. "Sir Samuel Garth, A Court Physician of the 18th Century." *Isis*, 29 (1938), 29-42. A brief, but good, account of Garth's career.

CUSHING, HARVEY. "Dr. Garth: The Kit-Kat Poet." *Bulletin of the Johns Hopkins Hospital*, 17 (1906), 1-17. Discussion of Garth's role in the medical and literary disputes of his day.

DWYER, WARREN F. "Profit, Poetry, and Politics in Augustan Translation: A Study of the Tonson-Garth *Metamorphoses* of 1717." Ph.D. dissertation, University of Illinois, 1969. An excellent account of the background of the Garth edition of Ovid and an assessment, mostly negative, of its literary quality.

ELLIS, FRANK H. "Garth's Harveian Oration." *Journal of the History of Medicine*, 18 (1963), 8-19. Prints and discusses Garth's English draft of his Latin oration.

———. "The Background of the London Dispensary." *Journal of the History of Medicine*, 20 (1965), 197-212. Discusses the historical context of the dispensary dispute.

HOPKINS, D. W. "Dryden's Cave of Sleep and Garth's *Dispensary.*" *Notes and Queries*, 23 (1976), 243-245. Suggests that Dryden's description of the Cave of Sleep in his translation of book 11 of Ovid's *Metamorphoses* (*Fables*, 1700) derives from Garth's portrait of sloth in *The Dispensary*.

JOHNSON, SAMUEL. "Life of Garth." In *The Lives of the English Poets*. 3 vols. Edited by George B. Hill. 1905; reprint ed., New York: Octagon Books, 1967. Garth's "Life" is in volume 2.

MCCUE, DANIEL L. "Samuel Garth, Physician and Man of Letters." *Bulletin of the New York Academy of Medicine*, 53 (1976), 368-402. A general account of Garth's life.

MOORE, NORMAN. "Sir Samuel Garth." In *The Dictionary of National Biography*. 22 vols. Edited by Leslie Stephen and Sidney Lee. London: Oxford University Press, 1921-1922. Garth's biography is in volume 7.

ROBERTS, PHILIP E. "The Background and Purpose of Garth's *Dispensary* (1699)." *Journal of the Royal College of Physicians of London*, 2 (1968), 154-60.

ROGERS, PAT. "The Publishing History of Garth's *Dispensary:* Some 'Lost' and Pirated editions." *Transactions of the Cambridge Bibliographical Society*, 5 (1971), 167-77. An unpedantic essay in bibliography.

ROSENBERG, ALBERT. "The Authorship of the Verses on Marlborough's Exile." *Notes and Queries*, 201 (1956), 429-30. Shows these verses, long attributed to Garth, are by George Sewell.

———. "The Sarah Stout Murder Case: An Early Example of the Doctor

Selected Bibliography

    as an Expert Witness." *Journal of the History of Medicine,* 12 (1957), 61-70. Garth's testimony in a Hertford trial.

———. "The London Dispensary for the Sick-Poor." *Journal of the History of Medicine,* 14 (1959), 41-56. Traces the apothecary-physician dispute before and after *The Dispensary.*

———. "The Last Days of Sir Samuel Garth: A Footnote to a Pope Letter." *Notes and Queries,* 204 (1959), 272-74. An account of Garth's deathbed stoicism.

SCHENK, THEODOR. *Sir Samuel Garth und Seine Stellung zum Komischen Epos.* Heidelberg: Carl Winter's Universitätsbuchhandlung, 1900. Primarily a comparison of parallels (some very tenuous) from *The Dispensary* and other works.

SCHNEIDER, DUANE B. "Words from Garth's *Dispensary.*" *Notes and Queries,* 208 (1963), 419. Additions from Garth for the *Oxford English Dictionary.*

———. "Dr. Garth and Shakespeare: A Borrowing." *English Language Notes,* 1 (1964), 200-202. Suggests similarities between Garth's description of Horoscope's shop and the apothecary's shop in *Romeo and Juliet.*

SENA, JOHN F. "Samuel Garth's *The Dispensary.*" *Texas Studies in Literature and Language,* 15 (1974), 639-48. Discussion of *The Dispensary* as a poem.

[SHIELLS, ROBERT]. *The Lives of the Poets of Great Britain and Ireland.* 5 vols. London: R. Griffiths, 1753. This work, which was wrongly credited to Theophilus Cibber, has a laudatory essay on Garth in volume 4.

Index

Accomplisht Physician, 51, 53, 145n
Adams, William, 64, 65
Addison, Joseph, 21, 23, 24, 28, 34, 35, 39, 44, 79, 83, 88, 96, 115, 116, 121, 129, 132, 142n, 149n, 154n, 155n, 160n; *Cato*, 10, 113, 114
Aitken, G. A., 143n
Allen, Robert J., 138n, 154n
Anderson, Robert, 127, 133, 158n
Andrews, Alexander, 140n
Anne, Queen of England, 21, 25, 28, 30, 32, 82, 107, 115, 116, 140n, 152n, 155n
Apothecaries, Society of the Art and Mystery of, 14, 46-59, 144n
Arbuthnot, Dr. John, 31, 38, 42, 143n
Argyll, Duke of, 28
Ariosto, 63
Aristotle, *De Poetica*, 62
Atterbury, Bishop Francis, 24
Audra, E., 139n, 151n
Ault, Norman, 142n
Ayre, William, 127, 158n

Bacon, Francis, 142n
Barber, John, 37
Barrett, C. R. B., 58, 144n, 145n
Bateman, Dr. John, 149n
Baugh, A. C., 160n
Beaufoy, Sir Henry, 9, 27
Beaumont, Thomas, 120
Bell, John, 119, 156n
Bennett, J. A. W., 147n
Bentley, Richard, 94, 95, 97, 152n
Berkeley, George, 23, 24, 32, 39, 141n, 142n, 143n
Bernard, Francis, 149n
Biographica Britannica, 120, 137n
Birch, Samuel, 149n
Bitzer, Lloyd, F., 150n

Blackmore, Sir Richard, 15, 16, 25, 60, 63, 73, 110, 125, 128, 130, 138n, 149n, 154n; *Discommendatory Verses*, 16, 110; *A Satyr Against Wit*, 16, 64, 96, 109, 153n
Blanchard, Rae, 143n, 152n
Bliss, John, 138n, 155n
Blount, Edward, 40
Blount, Henry, 16, 98, 146n
Blount, Martha, 33
Boileau-Despréaux, Nicolas, 73, 74, 76, 79, 129, 150n; *Le Lutrin*, 63-69, 78, 97, 146n, 147n
Bolton, Charles, 111
Bolton, Henrietta, 111
Bond, Donald F., 149n, 160n
Bond, Richmond P., 79, 97, 146n, 148n, 149n, 150n, 151n, 153n, 158n, 159n
Booth, Barton, 114
Boyer, Abel, 43, 65, 137n, 143n, 147n
Boyle, Charles (earl of Orrery), 16, 88, 94, 95, 97, 146n, 152n
Boyle, Henry, 27
Boyle, Robert, 145n
Boyle, Colonel William, 9, 27
Boys, Richard C., 138n, 140n, 154n, 158n
Bracegirdle, Anne, 113
Britton, W. Earl, 147n
Broome, William, 91
Brown, Tom, 19
Buchanan-Brown, John, 138n, 155n
Burgess, C. F., 153n
Burlington, Earl of, 111, 112
Bush, Douglas, 124, 158n
Butler, Samuel, *Hudibras*, 18, 43, 62, 132, 134, 150n
Butt, John, 139n, 142n, 157n, 159n
Bysshe, Edward, 87, 151n

166

Index

Cabrini, Sister Mary, 147n
Campbell, George, 84, 150n
Campion, Miss, 142n
Carlisle, Anne, 110
Carlos VI, Emperor of Spain, 115
Caroline, Princess of England, 122
Cartwright, J., 139n
Caryll, John, 114
Catling, Christopher, 21
Celsus, A. Cornelius, 81
Censor Censur'd, 58
Cervantes, Miguel de, *Don Quixote*, 20
Chalmers, Alexander, 138n, 140n, 143n, 145n, 146n, 147n, 149n, 150n, 151n, 152n, 153n, 154n, 155n, 156n, 157n
Charles I, King of England, 107
Charles II, King of England, 48, 144n
Charlett, Arthur, 150n
Charlton, John, 110
Chaucer, Geoffrey, 62
Cheek, Thomas, 87, 146n
Churchill, Charles, 21, 22, 126, 158n
Churchill, Winston S., 141n
Cibber, Theophilus, 153n
Clark, A. F. B., 66, 147n, 150n, 151n, 153n, 158n
Clark, George N., 144n
Clifford, James, 147n, 151n
Clive, Lord, 109
Codrington, Christopher, 146n
Collier, Jeremy, 112, 113
Commendatory Verses, 25, 109
Congreve, William, 20, 21, 35, 39, 83, 99, 112, 125, 147n
Cooke, John, 145n
Cornog, William H., 11, 137n, 141n, 153n
Courthope, William J., 75, 133, 149n, 160n
Coward, William, 99, 153n
Cowper, William, 160n
Coxe, Daniel, 49
Craggs, James, 24, 29, 34, 43
Crowne, John, 147n
Cushing, Harvey, 140n

Dalrymple, John, 36
Davis, Herbert, 141n, 152n

Dearing, Vinton, 155n, 160n
Defoe, Daniel, 64, 65, 125, 147n, 154n, 159n
Demosthenes, 120
Denham, Sir J., *Cooper's Hill*, 33, 100, 101, 107, 108
Dennis, John (Garth's contemporary), 16, 17, 81, 150n
Dennis, John (modern critic), 133, 158n, 160n
Devonshire, Duke of, 139n, 142n
Diffenbaugh, Guy L, 149n
Dingle, Miss, 26
Dispensary Transvers'd, 128
Dissertator in Burlesque, 96, 128, 153n
Dobreé, Bonamy, 133, 134, 140n, 160n
Dodsley, Robert, 139n
Dorset, Earl of, 21, 73
Drake, Dr. James, 25, 127
Drummond, John, 29
Dryden, John, 16, 17, 18, 19, 20, 35, 63, 69, 83, 88, 96, 103, 120, 121, 125, 126, 127, 132, 138n, 147n, 148n, 160n; *Absalom and Achitophel*, 69-74, 146n; *MacFlecknoe*, 62, 69-74, 130
Dunbar, William, *Turnament*, 62
Drayton, Michael, *Nymphidia*, 62
Dwyer, Warren F., 142n
Dwyer, William, 123, 124, 157n, 158n

Egmond, Earl of, 39, 142n
Elizabeth, Queen of England, 31
Ellis, Frank, 91, 92, 93, 133, 134, 137n, 138n, 144n, 145n, 146n, 147n, 149n, 150n, 152n, 153n, 156n, 158n, 159n, 160n
Elwin-Courthope, Whitwell, 159n
Epistle to Sr. Richard Blackmore, 20, 125
Epistle to Sir Samuel Garth, 35
Epistles of Phalaris, 94, 95
Escal, Françoise, 147n
Essex, Lord, 21
Essex, Mary, 110
Eusden, Laurence, 103, 158n
Eves, C. K., 140n

Examiner, 27, 30

Farmer, John, S., 140n
Farquhar, George, 18, 138n
Fenton, Elijah, 91
Fermanagh, Viscount, 23
Fitzroy, Charles, 44
Fleischmann, Wolfgang B., 156n, 157n
Ford, Charles, 140n
Friedman, Arthur, 152n

Gardiner, Thomas, 149n
Garrod, H. W., 94, 152n
Garth, Martha (daughter), 9, 26, 27
Garth, Martha (wife), 9, 10, 27, 38
Garth, Samuel
WORKS:
"Anacreontic Epistle to Mr. Gay", 20, 117
Claremont, 10, 33, 99–109
Demosthenes, "First Philippick" (trans.), 9, 20, 118, 120
The Dispensary, 9, 10, 14, 15, 17, 20, 22, 24, 25, 29, 46–74, 75–98, 108–18, 126, 129, 132, 133, 134, 135, 161n
"Epilogue to the Tragedy of *Cato*," 10, 113, 114
Epitaphium Lucretii Editionis (trans.), 9, 120, 121, 141n
Eulogy at Dryden's funeral, 9, 17, 18, 19, 38, 118
"An Imitation of a French Author," 117
Letters of Samuel Garth, 138n, 140n, 141n, 143n, 144n
"On Her Majesty's Statue in St. Paul's Church-Yard," 29, 115, 116, 117, 118, 140n
"On the King of Spain," 25, 114, 115
"On the New Conspiracy, 1716," 35, 115, 117
Oratio Laudatoria in Aedibus Collegii Regalis Med. Lond., 13, 14, 57, 96, 118, 119, 121, 145n, 156n
Ovid, *Metamorphoses* (trans.), 10, 17, 35, 40, 99, 107, 118, 121, 122, 123, 124, 157n, 158n
Plutarch, *Life of Otho* (trans.), 9, 20, 118, 120
"Prologue Spoken at the Opening of the Queen's Theatre in the Haymarket," 25, 113
"Prologue to *Squire Trelooby*," 25, 112
"Prologue to *Tamerlane*," 25, 112
"Prologue to the Music-Meeting in the York Buildings," 117
"De Respiratione" (Gustonian Lecture), 9, 13
"A Soliloquy Out of Italian," 117
"To the Duchess of Bolton, On Her Staying All the Winter in The Country," 111
"To the Earl of Godolphin," 26, 114, 115
"To the Lady Louisa Lenos: With Ovid's Epistles," 111
"To the Merry Poetaster at Sadlers-Hall in Cheapside," 16, 109, 110, 154n
"Verses Written for the Toasting-Glasses of the Kit-kat Club, in the Year 1703," 110

Garth, Thomas (brother), 11
Garth, William (brother), 11
Garth, William (father), 9, 11
Gay, John, 20, 35, 99, 117, 118, 153n, 155n, 160n
Gaye, A. S., 142n
Gelsthorpe, Peter, 149n
Gentleman's Magazine, 153n, 158n
George I, King of England, 10, 25, 30, 32, 34, 36, 117, 118, 121
George, Prince of Denmark, 25
Gibbons, Dr. William, 149n
Gill, Dr. Thomas, 149n
Gildon, Charles, 20, 158n
Gilmore, Thomas, 138n
Goddard, Jonathan, 49
Godolphin, Earl of, 9, 26, 27, 28, 29, 115, 116
Gold, Dr. William, 149n
Goldsmith, Oliver, 93, 152n
Goodall, Dr. Charles, 149n
Gosse, Edmund, 133, 160n
Granby, Lady, 110
Grant, Douglas, 158n
Grantham, Lord, 25

Index

Granville, George, 36, 141n
Green, David, 139n
Greene, G. W., 155n
Grierson, Sir Herbert, 152n
Grocers Company, 15, 46
Guthrie, William, 126

Hall, Joseph, 80
Hallam, Henry, 132, 152n, 160n
Halley, Dr. Edmund, 39
Halsband, Robert, 143n
Hamilton, Duke of, 28
Hamilton, General Hans, 29
Hancock, Dr. John, 143n
Harley, Robert (earl of Oxford), 28, 29, 114
Harris, Bruce, 154n
Harte, Walter, 20, 138n, 148n
Harvey, William, 13, 48, 61, 67, 119, 138n, 146n
Hayley, William, 127, 158n
Haymarket Theatre, 113
Hearne, Thomas, 18, 39, 118, 138n, 142n, 155n
Henley, W. E., 140n
Henry VIII, King of England, 46
Hewet, Frances, 44
Higgons, Sir Thomas, 36
Hill, George B., 149n, 150n, 151n, 152n, 155n, 156n, 157n
Hinton, Edward, 18, 118
Hodges, Dr. Nathaniel, 49, 144n
Hooker, E. N., 150n
Homer, 62, 63, 79, 129; *Iliad*, 77, 78, 81
Howe, Dr. George, 149n
Hutchenson, Francis, 24
Hyde, Jane, 110

Inese, Lewis, 34
Irving, William H., 124, 138n, 154n, 158n

Jack, Ian, 87, 150n, 159n
Jacob, Giles, 41, 143n
James II, King of England, 12, 14, 144n
Jebb, R. C., 94, 152n
Jenyns, Soames, 151n
Jervas, Charles, 40
Jessop, T. E., 141n

Johnson, Samuel, *Lives of the English Poets*, 75, 80, 88, 90, 100, 116, 120, 127, 138n, 149n, 150n, 151n, 152n, 153n, 155n, 156n, 157n
Jones, Richard F., 152n
Jones, W. P., 150n
Jonson, Ben, 147n
Juvenal, 81

Kenrick, Daniel, 43, 143n
Ker, W. P., 147n
Killigrew, Thomas, 41, 91, 143n, 152n
King, Lester, 160n
King, William, 128
Kingsley, James, 138n, 148n
Kit-Cat Club, 9, 20, 21, 38, 100, 110, 111, 113, 154n, 155n
Knapp, Mary E., 154n
Kneller, Godfrey, 43
Knox, Vicesimus, 127, 158n

Lacy, John, 43, 143n
Lamoignon M. de, 64
Landa, Lewis A., 143n, 147n, 151n
Leblanc, Abbé François, 96, 97
Lee, Sidney, 152n, 154n
Leicht, William J., 146n, 161n
Lenos, Charles (duke of Richmond), 111
Lenos, Louisa, 111
Leslie, Charles, 113
Lewis, R. W., 151n
Lex Talionis, 50, 144n
Leyden, University of, 11
Lintot, Bernard, 34, 118
London Post Boy, 15
Louis XIV, King of France, 67, 112, 120
Luce, A. A., 141n
Lucretius, 30
Luttrell, Narcissus, 139n

Macaulay, Lord Thomas B., 94, 114, 152n, 154n
Mainwaring, Arthur, 25
Malone, Edmund, 16, 19, 138n
Manuscripts of the House of Lords, 137n
Mar, Duke of, 34, 36

Marlborough, Duchess of, 21, 22, 23, 29, 43
Marlborough, Duke of, 9, 12, 21, 22, 23, 24, 28, 29, 31, 32, 42, 43, 114, 116, 117, 141n, 154n, 155n
Mary, Queen of England, 155n
Masham, Lord, 31
Mason, William, 151n
Maynwaring, Everard, 50, 158n
Medice Cura Teipsum, 50
Medley, 28, 140n
Menzies, John, 34
Merrett, Dr. Christopher, 49, 50, 145n
Milford, H. S., 160n
Miller, Frank Justus, 123, 157n
Miller, H. K., 143n
Millington, Sir Thomas, 149n, 152n
Milton, John, 127; *Paradise Lost,* 78, 79
Miner, Earl, 160n
Mist's Weekly Journal, 87
Moliere, Jean Baptiste, 112
Montagu, M. F. A., 145n
Montagu, Charles (Lord Halifax), 156n
Montagu, Lady Mary Wortley, 25, 43, 44, 143n
Moore, Norman, 111, 154n
Motteux, Pierre, 20
Mullett, Charles F., 144n
Munk, William, 11, 137n, 156n
Murphy, Arthur, 85

Necessity and Usefulness, 58
Nichols, John, 151n
Nicolson, Marjorie, 143n
Nutt, John, 20

"Occasion'd by the Death of Dr. Garth," 37
Oldham, John, 147n
Oldmixon, John, 121, 140n, 157n
Original Weekly Journal, 38
Osborn, James M., 137n, 139n, 147n, 149n, 151n
Overbury, Sir Thomas, 80
Ovid, *Metamorphoses,* 10, 81, 100, 105, 106, 111, 121, 157n
Ozell, John, 65

Pack, Richardson, 152n
Palmer, Ralph, 23
Pelham-Holles, Thomas (earl of Clare, duke of Newcastle), 33, 35, 36, 100, 101, 102, 103, 109, 141n, 153n
Perceval, Sir John, 32
Peterborough, Earl of, 140n
Phillips, Steven R., 77, 147n, 149n
Pierce, Edward, 149n
Pierce, Michael, 149n
Pierrepont, William, 43
Pinkus, Philip, 138n
Pitt, Robert, 58
Playford, Henry, 19
Plutarch, *Lives of the Noble Grecians and Romans,* 120
Pope, Alexander, 12, 23, 24, 33, 35, 37, 40, 44, 70, 73, 76, 84, 88, 90, 91, 114, 122, 127, 128, 129, 130, 131, 132, 139n, 141n, 142n, 149n, 150n, 151n, 152n, 154n, 156n, 157n, 158n, 159n, 160n; *The Dunciad,* 129, 130, 131, 133, 134; *Essay on Criticism,* 90, 147n; *Letter to a Noble Lord,* 129; *Pastorals,* 23; *Rape of the Lock,* 23, 73, 127, 129, 133, 134; *Windsor Forest,* 33, 100, 101, 105, 107, 108
Porter, Mary, 114
Post Boy, 17, 57, 118
Powell, Thomas, 73
Present Ill State, 58
Previté-Orton, C. W., 155n
Prior, Matthew, 21, 27, 30, 111, 115, 116, 140n, 155n
Prophetic Physician, 131
Pulteney, Arabelle, 27

Ralph, John, 154n
Reade, Aleyn, L., 151n
Resnel, Jean du, 150n
Richardson, Jonathan, 91, 152n
Roberts, Philip E., 138n, 142n, 144n, 145n, 149n, 154n
Rogers, Pat, 134, 161n
Root, Robert K., 160n
Roper, Abel, 19
Rose, William, 59

Index

Rosen, George, 145n
Rosenberg, Albert, 139n, 142n, 144n, 145n, 155n
Rothstein, E., 143n
Rousseau, G. S., 143n
Rowe, Nicholas, 35, 63, 65, 96, 112, 125
Royal College of Physicians, 9, 12, 13, 14, 24, 46-59, 77, 144n; *Annals*, 12, 17, 48, 55, 144n
Royal Commission on Historical Manuscripts, 137n, 138n, 139n 155n
Royal Society, 9, 24

Sackville, Charles (earl of Dorset), 154n
St. Batholomew's Hospital, 51
St. John, Henry (Viscount Bolingbroke), 10, 28, 33, 34, 35, 44, 141n
St. Mary's Church, Harrow-on-the-Hill, 10, 38
St. Thomas's Hospital, 51
Saintsbury, George, 70, 88, 89, 91, 133, 148n, 151n, 152n
Sandys, George, 122
Schenk, Theodor, 26, 65, 66, 140n, 147n, 159n
Schmidt, Karlernst, 97, 153n, 156n
Scott, Sir Walter, 31, 141n, 154n
Sedley, Sir Charles, 16
Sena, John F., 138n, 150n, 157n
Sewell, Dr. George, 154n
Sherburn, George, 134, 139n, 152n, 154n, 160n
Shiells, Robert, 108, 121, 153n, 157n
Shippen, William, 156n
Shirley, James, 113
Sloane, Sir Hans, 21, 22, 24, 27, 42, 56, 139n
Smith, Benjamin, 142n
Smith, N. Nichol, 140n
Smith, F. Seymour, 124, 158n
Somers, Lord, 21, 61, 152n, 153n
Somerset, Lord, 21
Spanish Succession, War of, 28, 31, 112

Spears, M. K., 155n
Spence, Joseph, 39, 44, 65, 151n, 156n; *Anecdotes*, 37, 40, 139n, 142n, 143n, 149n
State of Physick, 58
State Papers, 12
Steele, Sir Richard, 16, 21, 24, 28, 41, 44, 93, 114, 125, 143n, 149n, 152n, 160n
Stephen, Leslie, 152n, 154n
Stock, Joseph, 39
Stonehill, Charles, 138n
Story of the St. Alban's Ghost, 31, 38, 109
Stratford, Dr. William, 28
Straus, Ralph, 138n
Studley Royal, 108
Sunderland, Lord, 21
Surtees, Robert, 137n
Sutherland, James, 159n
Swift, Jonathan, 24, 30, 37, 140n, 141n, 142n, 152n, 154n, 159n, 160n; *Journal to Stella*, 30, 31, 140n

Tanner, Thomas, 64
Tasso, 63
Tassoni, Alessandro, 62, 63
Tate, Nahum, 158n
Temple, Sir William, 94, 95, 152n
Tentamen Medicinale, 58
Thornton, Bonnell, 131
Tillotson, Geoffrey, 84, 129, 133, 150n, 151n, 159n, 160n
Timbs, J., 143n
"To Richard Earl of Burlington," 111, 112
Tonson, Jacob, 20, 21, 24, 35, 100, 110, 121, 122, 139n, 142n, 157n
Townley, Mr., 37, 44
Toynbee, Paget, 158n
Trevelyan, Lady, 152n, 154n
Tryal of Skill, 125
Tyson, Dr. Edward, 54, 145n, 149n

Underwood, Ashworth, 144n, 145n
Utrecht, Peace of, 32, 116

Villette, Marquise de, 35

Vanbrugh, John, 21, 100, 109, 112, 113, 139n, 140n, 154n
Vergil, 17, 63, 78, 79, 100, 104
Vernon, James, 122, 157n
Voltaire, 65, 127, 147n

Walker, Hugh, 146n, 161n
Waller, A. R., 148n, 152n
Waller, Edmund, 62, 108
Walpole, Horace, 126, 151n, 158n
Walsh, William, 16, 112
Ward, A. W., 148n, 152n
Ward, Ned, 18, 58, 125, 138n, 145n
Ward, Thomas H., 151n
Warren, Austin, 133, 160n
Warton, Joseph, 41, 65, 73, 83, 143n, 147n, 150n, 157n
Watkins, Henry, 29
Webb, Geoffrey, 140n

Weekly Journal, 38
Weekly Medley, 38
Weekly Packet, 38, 42, 44
Wesley, Samuel, 79
Wharton, Earl of, 25, 139n, 140n
Wharton, Lady Anne, 110
Wilkinson, L. P., 124, 158n
William III, King of England, 12, 13, 14, 67, 96, 97, 107, 108, 112, 119, 152n, 153n
Williams, A., 139n, 151n
Williams, Harold, 140n, 142n, 152n, 160n
Williams, Sir William, 56
Wolcot, John, *The Louisiad*, 131
Wright, H. B., 155n
Wycherly, William, 20, 83

Young, Edward, 39